Cold War

The Cold War's Most Remarkable Operation

(Adventures From the Coldest Part of the Cold War)

Trent Thompson

Published By **Andrew Zen**

Trent Thompson

All Rights Reserved

Cold War: The Cold War's Most Remarkable Operation (Adventures From the Coldest Part of the Cold War)

ISBN 978-1-77485-567-6

No part of this guidebook shall be reproduced in any form without permission in writing from the publisher except in the case of brief quotations embodied in critical articles or reviews.

Legal & Disclaimer

The information contained in this ebook is not designed to replace or take the place of any form of medicine or professional medical advice. The information in this ebook has been provided for educational & entertainment purposes only.

The information contained in this book has been compiled from sources deemed reliable, and it is accurate to the best of the Author's knowledge; however, the Author cannot guarantee its accuracy and validity and cannot be held liable for any errors or omissions. Changes are periodically made to this book. You must consult your doctor or get professional medical advice before using any of the suggested remedies, techniques, or information in this book.

Upon using the information contained in this book, you agree to hold harmless the Author from and against any damages, costs, and expenses, including any legal fees potentially resulting from the application of any of the information provided by this guide. This disclaimer applies to any damages or injury caused by the use and application, whether directly or indirectly, of any advice or information presented, whether for breach of contract, tort, negligence, personal injury, criminal intent, or under any other cause of action.

You agree to accept all risks of using the information presented inside this book. You need to consult a professional medical practitioner in order to ensure you are both able and healthy enough to participate in this program.

TABLE OF CONTENTS

Introduction 1

Chapter 1: Berlin The Lines Have Been Drawn 6

Chapter 2: Stemming The Tide Of Communism In East Asia 16

Chapter 3: Fight Space With Soviets In The Fight For Supremacy In Space 28

Chapter 4: How Cold War Calculus Affected The Middle East 49

Chapter 5: Cuba, Vietnam, And Growing Social Unrest 60

Chapter 6: A East African Cold War 91

Chapter 7: Cold War Secrets And A Place Called Area 51 101

Chapter 8: Soviets, Afghanistan, And A Bit Of Salt 116

Chapter 9: Ronald Reagan And The Evil Empire 123

Chapter 10: The Early Definition Of Events 136

Chapter 11: Major Events And Battlegrounds . 145

Chapter 12: Themes Of Major Themes............ 161

Chapter 13: The Collapse Of The Soviet Bloc... 177

Conclusion 182

Introduction

Seeds of the Cold War were planted at the end of World War II. The conflict was a time when it was clear that the United States and the Soviet Union were reluctant accomplices. The socialist ideology from the Soviets was at odds with the US views of private business, free enterprise as well as rough independence. As is the case in every situation despite their differences, America and Soviet Russia had a common enemy that brought them together: Nazi Germany.

So the moment that Germany's adversary, Imperial Japan, assaulted the US and put the nation to an impact course in conjunction with Japan, the Axis Powers of Germany, Japan and Italy It was normal that Americans were forced to join in the direction of the Soviet Union, which was in the process of being brought to a standstill by Nazi developments throughout Eastern Europe. It was due to efforts to defeat this Axis which American doubts regarding Soviet theology were removed. Additionally, during the war, American President Franklin Delano Roosevelt actually ended up in a truly great relationship along with Soviet head, Joseph Stalin.

In the course of the war system gatherings or culminatings as they were known in the presence of FDR and Stalin as the two seemed to develop close to each other. It was a bond that British Premier Winston Churchill viewed as upsetting because Churchill immediately realized that a conflict among the Soviets and the free Europe was likely to arise after the war's end.

Residents of Roosevelt suddenly passed away in the month of April 1945. He did not live to witness the end of World War II. When American representative William Averell Harriman was able to educate Stalin on the passing of FDR, Stalin was said to appear to be sad. In tears Stalin, the socialist dictator realizing Harry Truman was next up for consideration by the administration, in unison declared "President Roosevelt has kicked the bucket, but his motives will live on. We will stand up for the presidency of President Truman with all our power and with all of our will."

However, before Truman was in charge of his administration in Truman's administration in the

United States, American and Soviet relations quickly began to decline. After the war was done, conflict arose about how the postbellum world was to be managed. The primary dispute was about the principal enemy of the war--the destroyed Axis forces that was Nazi Germany.

In May 1945 America along with her British partner had joined forces to enlarge Germany together with Soviet Russia, a partnership that would turn into a separate segment based on philosophical considerations. A part of Germany was controlled by the other.

Russians are the main beneficiaries, and it will be socialist. The other one would be governed by the Allies as well as provide a refuge for the majority rule capitalism. One of the major issues in this war was the massive flooding of German exiles from the Soviet region towards their homeland in the American zone. It was a time when the Soviets and Germans faced a violent conflict that resulted in destruction on both sides. A large portion of the German population, realizing the Americans were more friendly occupiers than Russians fled to on the American side.

The Russians required to stop this and demanded that the Americans remove refuge seekers. However, American military leaders regularly did not coordinate. Through the end of 1940 in the 1940s, there was a Soviet Union had introduced manikin legislatures throughout Eastern Europe, including what could eventually being East Germany. The time of social unification is one of the two in which Winston Churchill caught very well when he delivered his famous "Iron

Curtain" Discourse, also known as"the "Ligaments of Peace" on March 5 1946. In this speech, in where the president Harry Truman himself was in presence, Churchill broadly proclaimed that the iron curtain of oppression was falling across Europe due to Soviet control. Churchill's American friends, who were at the time in conflict with the Soviets were able to take the speech seriously. However, the Soviet Union, obviously, did not. In any event Churchill's speech was not an appeal to war, but as much it was a information about the events that were rapidly unfolding after the end of the war.

Churchill was adamant, "From Stettin in the Baltic from Stettin in the Baltic to Trieste to Trieste in the Adriatic An iron curtain is falling across the continent. Behind that line lies all cities in the old regions that comprise Central as well as Eastern Europe. Warsaw, Berlin, Prague, Vienna, Budapest, Belgrade, Bucharest, and Sofia This large collection of well-known urban communities as well as the people who live there are in what I refer to as the Soviet circle. All are subject to some sort of arrangement, but not only to Soviet impacts, but to a very large and sometimes growing proportion of influence from Moscow." Churchill's speech confirmed what many officials in the administration of both the East as well as the West were feeling. Within a year of the end of the blazes in World War II had been extinguished the cold chill of a new, long-lasting struggle began to fill the air. It was the time for war. Cold War had begun.

Chapter 1: Berlin The Lines Have Been Drawn

"Communism is a method to think about discontent, the declaration of faith in the obliviousness of others, and the joy of jealousy. Its ethical foundation is the corresponding sharing of the pain."

Winston Churchill

This city in Berlin is traced all the way through its beginnings in the Middle Ages and has for long been seen as possibly the most vibrant and sophisticated European city in all likelihood in the course of World War II. Tragically, Berlin, just like the rest of Germany was taken over by the Nazi Nazi Party. This once-thriving group of writers music, arts, and crafts was betrayed by the savagery and savagery of Adolf Hitler. However, even after the demise of Hitler on the 30th April 1945, Berlin's troubles were not being over.

The immediate repercussions in World War II, Berlin was involved in a mutually beneficial way by The United States and the Soviet Union and effectively divided the city into two. Germany was at present been divided between East and West, but from the vast majority of urban communities that existed in Germany Berlin's situation was the most difficult to navigate since the entire city was in Soviet-involved territory.

While West Berlin would stay liberated from Soviet control but it was an area of a vote-based system which was bound up by the socialist-based ideology that was the norm in East Germany. The Soviets continued to maintain their control over Berlin for the majority of the of Cold War, ultimately fabricating an unidirectional divide through Berlin and later, some. But, perhaps among the most terrifying and thrilling moments of the Berlin impasse throughout the Cold War happened in the late spring of 1947 in the midst of the rumored Berlin Airlift also known as Berliner Luftbrucke or Berliner Luftbrucke in German ("Berlin Air Bridge"). At that point the regions of Germany that were being restricted to The United States, Britain, and France had merged to form a single entity called West Germany. America was working to turn West Germany into a prosperous nation, while the Soviets were pushing socialist rules into the lives of East Germans. This was a serious flashpoint, and the situation was dire.

It was a critical moment in the 24th of June, 1948 that was the day when the Soviets blocked the roads and railroad lines that allowed access to the west side of Berlin. The reason for this was a result of the fact about the Allies had set up a new Deutsche Mark money related cash in West Germany. The Soviets opposed this. Following World War II had found one conclusion. Soviet leader Joseph Stalin didn't want for an economically viable Germany to rise up again. In the present

That the Western powers were aiding in rebuilding economies in West Germany, in addition to the fact that there financial strength was returning within West Germany, yet it also sparked Stalin's fear that any West German financial achievement would cause East Germany wish to stick to the same model. Stalin realized that this could weaken his reliance on the Soviet-controlled sector.

In a slick attempt to make the world aware of their displeasure they made the Soviets immediately revoked access to Berlin. This was an extremely anger towards the Soviets because it could be the cause of a staged confrontation between American as well as Russian soldiers. It also appeared to do nothing but head towards that direction because a lot of tactical pioneers had been by sending escorts in uniformed escorts through the blocked streets to break an Soviet blockade. However, rather than take chances with the deadlock, a different option was thrown out. While thinking about the situation from a different angle the military leaders began to consider what their options really were. In the end, it seemed right. If they were unable to get to Berlin via air, why couldn't they do it via air? This is how the idea of the Berlin Airlift - a plan to transport fuel, food and medical supplies by air

about. The airdrop began in force on June 26 1948, and America along with her Western partners began dropping their freights across the town. It was an incredible feat that, at a particular time, nearly 13,000 tons of supplies were transported each day.

The activities officially ended in mid-year 1949, after the Soviets had completed their barricade on the overland routes that led up to West Berlin. That being stated that there was a resurgence of the Western Allies kept on dropping items via air in case the Soviets tried to block the overland route once again. Therefore, the transporter was not really brought completely to an end until the autumn of 1949. It was a painful deadlock with stakes higher than what was commonly thought.

The United States and its partners were in a weak position within Western Europe. After the end in World War II, the strategic existence of Western partners had drastically reduced. The soldiers, of course, wanted to be reunited with their families. And, after the war was supposedly over there was only a skeleton team that remained was comprised of two to three hundred thousand people. But it was the case that the Soviets never really reduced their strength, and had over 1 million soldiers trained and ready. In the event that they were to launch an attack, Soviets were to swiftly launch an attack and the Western defense forces would have been crushed.

But it was the United States had the atomic secret weapon. The US provided the world's very first Atomic bomb during the latter portion of World War II,

Inaugurating the atomic age the dropping of two nuclear bombs at Japan during 1945. The Soviets knew without doubt they had an atomic arsenal. United States had an atomic armory, but were skeptical whether they would make use of it. The year 1948 was the time when coordination of an effective nuclear attack against an opponent in the USSR (Union of Soviet Socialist Republics) would be difficult.

this was prior to the introduction to ICBMs (intercontinental Long Range Rockets) that means that the attack would have to be carried out in the same way to the bombing of Japan. This meant using large aircraft planes to transport the weapons across Russian airspace, and then dropping the nuclear bombs from the plane. This hefty plan would have been extremely difficult in ideal circumstances. However, because the Russians had a formidable air defence, the likelihood of an aircraft being able to go to fall before they could launch their nuclear weapons was extremely large.

However the fact is, it was a possibility that however, it was a decision that President Harry S. Truman considered and proved when he dispatched B-29 planes to Britain and asked them to stay on reserve in case the decision was made to launch a bombing flight. It was enough of a reason to allow Stalin think about any other threats, especially since the Soviets would not make their nuclear first weapon until the 29th of August the 29th of August, 1949.

In the Berlin Airlift, the lines of the Cold War had become unmistakably drawn. This was the time which was when the North Atlantic Treaty Organization (NATO) was created. The Divine has arranged from the heavens a coordinated effort to aid Western nations despite Soviet threat. Following The Berlin Airlift found some conclusion, West Germany was authoritatively thought of as"the "Government Republic of Germany." The following year, the Soviets tackled this issue by creating the claimed "German Democratic Republic" out of the Soviet-controlled East Germany.

Because East Germany was turning out to be a bit isolated from the rest in the globe, West Germany turned out to be more integrated with it's European neighbors. The closer ties between Western nations were deemed to be crucial in order to stand firm against Soviet growth and serve as a means to help in preventing any future threats to Western Europe. NATO was certainly a part of this, but so was the creation of the European Coal and Steel Community (ECSC) that was, in a variety of ways, created the foundations for what could eventually become what would eventually become the European Union (EU).

In 1951 in 1951, the Treaty of Paris fixed the financial destiny for West Germany,

France, Italy, Luxembourg, Belgium, and Holland all in unison, without precedent in history. The ECSC that was put in place by this document was able to show fortitude in spite of Soviet tensions. It was also believed that the more economically interconnected the nations from Western Europe were, the more outrageous they'd be when they took to the streets against each other later. In the case of this book in the decade of 2020 this theory has proven to be correct. Albeit Western Europe had been the area of innumerable conflicts between Europeans previously-- including two universal conflicts-- from that day forward, there has not been any mobilized animosity between the countries of Western

Europe. They are closer than at any other period in recent history. Eastern Europe has seen struggle since World War II, yet Western Europe has not.

It is crucial to note that, even in the event that Ukraine participates in a dispute with Russia in the 2020s and beyond, the Ukrainians attempt to join forces and grit with European Union. Theyalso may want to benefit from the security of territorial and financial that the EU provides. It was during the beginning of Cold War that the European Union was first conceived and was apportioned West Germany being its easternmost border.

While this was happening in the meantime, it was also the case that Soviet Union was supporting its own blend of Eastern European states via otherwise called the anticipate, created at Warsaw, Poland. This was a pact that brought all the Eastern Bloc nations of Poland, Romania, Hungary, East Germany, Czechoslovakia, Bulgaria and Albania in order to create an overall security plan for the region.

Western authorities believed that the Warsaw Pact to be to an extent futile, as the Soviets had previously had agreements which were reviewed with all of the countries involved. However they Soviets were keen to provide an emotional response to the world by demonstrating that they had a fully-equipped with a camp Eastern European socialists to go face-to-face with the Western camp should they were to decide to strike. With NATO as well as an early stage of EU organization as well as the Warsaw Pact set up, the boundaries between the Cold War had been plainly drawn. The supposed "Warsaw Pact." "The Warsaw Pact,

Warsaw Treaty Organization, was in fact, as one could imagine.

Chapter 2: Stemming The Tide Of Communism In East Asia

"Assuming you must know the taste of a pears You should alter the flavor of the pear through drinking it. If you're required to know the theory and the techniques to deal with disturbance, you must participate in the transformation. The only way to be sure that you are able to verify information is through the direct encounter."

Mao Zedong

as the fate as the fate of Western Europe, the situation in East Asia before long happened to be a source of concern throughout in the Cold War. Even prior to the time that World War II had authoritatively reached a conclusion, China was in the process of fighting against the Japanese as it fought their individual Civil War. The two main sides of this war was the China Nationalists led by Chiang Kai-shek and the Communists that were ruled through Mao Zedong. While the Communists faced the more obvious risk of being defeated by Japan There were moments of collaboration between the two sides, however these were not permanent break in their battle against one another.

The Nationalists were the most burdened as they were the main military force that took on Japan. While the Communists were generally kept in remote districts relying on guerilla warfare and guerilla warfare, China's Nationalist forces were on the streets, fighting it out against Japan. Meanwhile, Mao Zedong and different Communists were mostly protected and hunkered down in the mountains.

The Nationalists could beat the Japanese eventually, but because they had taken on too much of the battle their strength had dramatically reduced. Mao was waiting to take advantage of his chance and bolstering the power that was his Red Army. Following the defeat of Japan what was left was Mao's Nationalists as well as Mao's Red Army would eventually go into a situation of hard and rapid war with each other in mid-year 1946. In spite of Mao's mathematical advantages and his mathematical prowess, the Nationalists had better equipment and equipment, since a large portion of the equipment Mao's Communists employed was outdated and outdated. Even though the Soviets were clearly in support of the Communists but they still would not want to create the trouble of supplying weapons to Mao.

After the end the second half of World War II, the Soviets had delayed announcing war on Japan and had sent troops into the area that was previously Japanesecontrolled Manchuria in the northeastern region of China. With Japan's consent, Japanese military equipment came into the Soviets in their possession and they gave the equipment to Mao's army. Mao's recently-equipped soldiers were then able to strike

against against the Nationalists. It was a difficult fight, but the Chinese Communists ultimately won the upper hand and defeated the Nationalists completely off the island.

What remains of the Nationalists were seeking asylum within the island of Taiwan and there they set up an interim government on Taiwan's Taiwanese capital city Taipei. The government based out of Taipei is referred to as an organization called the Republic of China, or the ROC and this body continues to exist up until the present day. The ROC was established in the meantime. Mao Zedong proclaimed triumph on the 1st of October, 1949.

indicating the foundation that was the foundation People's Republic of China, the socialist government which actually is in charge of central China to this day.

The effects from the Chinese Civil War are frequently overlooked, but it was akin to the division between East as well as West Germany, the segment of North and South Korea, and Vietnam. In reality, like these States, Taiwan was (and still is) an outgrowth of the Cold War's philosophies that were threatening. It was the Cold War was a polarizing time that divided people into 2 groups. It was either socialist or not.

Taiwan is in essence one of the Chinese area that separated from the central region in order to become a region free from Marxist doctrine. Prior to when the Japanese were able to take over Taiwan the territory was a part of China for quite a long time. But after the Japanese exiled and the Nationalists having no other place to turn, they created Taiwan their own place. Even though

Chiang Kai Shek's grip on the station may have been an unreliable one, since the man was able to escape the central region in a hurry, Taiwan has become a province player due to its own efforts and is now the most prosperous nation in the world.

The achievements by China's Chinese Communists on the central region, and their claims of being an authoritative socialist state aligned to the Soviet Union was of profound concern for those in the Western powers. They immediately sought to limit the threat, should socialism smudges the entire region aspects of East Asia. Their determination to stop spreading socialism was tested its first test of significance in the summer of 1950 when the socialist North Korea sent its soldiers into Western-held South Korea.

Korea had recently been a piece of the Japanese Empire, yet with Japan's loss, the Korean Peninsula had been split between the Western Allies and the Soviets, making a socialist moved system in the north and an entrepreneur/majority rule government in the south. These were the domains that were is isolated in the 38th Equal. Much like Germany, Korea had been divided and divided in accordance with the ideologies of two camps. North Korea, which was inspired by China's economic prosperity was convinced that it could get the ability to pursue an unconstrained union under one socialist Korean system.

In any event in any case, in any case, the United States was not going to stop for a moment and allow the situation to take place. The former President Harry Truman expressed at that time, "Assuming we let Korea down, the Soviets will continue to eat up one placeafter another." Considering the animosity that had been brewing, the newly negotiated United Nations gave power to the United States and Britain to stop the assault. US and British powerhouses have arrived on South Korea presently and immediately defeated North Koreans. North Koreans.

Even though there was a possibility that United States and its partners could have pushed their North Koreans back, because of an inexhaustible stock line of as well China as well as that of the Soviet Union, the North Koreans weren't likely to surrender anytime soon. In spite of the arms,

Chinese were also sneaking their own soldiers across the border, causing issues even more. In the wake of these snares Americans were anticipating that a greater conflict between China as well as Russia Soviet Union could arise, and they wanted to end the dispute as soon as possible.

The war would continue with a standstill for a few years, till a peace treaty was reached on July 31, 1953. The agreement created a two-mile-wide cradle zone , known by the name of DMZ (neutral territorial area) that was shared between North as well as South Korea. It is interesting that since there was there was no peace treaty in the DMZ, it was revealed that the Korean War never in fact was over, making it the longest-running peace treaty in history.

Following three decades of fighting five million people died which included around 4000 Americans. Although the Allies were able for averting the rise of communism they gained nothing. The truth is that neither side actually gained anythingsince the world basically returned to the way that it was prior to the gore began. Whatever the case the manner in which those in the Western powers, in particular America were able to end this limiting socialism was without certainty a victory for the US during the Cold War against the Soviets.

In the meantime, a new president was in the White House as President Dwight D. Eisenhower. Eisenhower was an Republican was previously an general in the armed forces as well as the Allied overseer of the war in Europe. Just a month after Eisenhower was appointed as the president of the United States, Soviet Premier Joseph Stalin died. Stalin was the Russian name that he

The name he chose for himself, which means "Man of Steel," was a sign to all the people of this world that he was not immortal regardless of what he chose to call himself. He slipped away erratically from the massive cerebral drain that led to stroke.

In the 1950s, an additional East Asian country was taking amazing steps. It wasn't toward socialism but rather towards an extremely efficient form of financial freedom enterprise. This was Japan. The uncongruity during Japan and the Cold War was a definitive adversary from both the United States during World War II. Both Japan and Germany were swiftly returned after their defeat. When they were restored, they were able to send guide to the US in the new war with the Soviets.

After their defeat after their defeat, neither Germany or Japan could have any military. However, the political value of the former adversaries with strong majority rule states with strong economies was hugely valuable. The more attractive West Germany looked, the more it did to make East Germany and the Soviet Union appear shabby. Similar was the case in the case of East Asia. The more successful Japan did under the direction of entrepreneurs and how much it failed to make the flimsier North Korea look inferior.

The success of Japan was itself an issue for the media in the 1950s, and by then in the 1950s, in the 1950s, the United States was emptying all it could from the East Asian country to ensure that it prospered. They viewed it as "the "Japanese miracle," but US support was a significant factor to have to do with the success. It was the United States realized that a happy and prosperous Japanese populace was more than willing to embrace extremeism or socialism. Additionally being a strong US forces in the district even with a robust Japanese economy, acted as a guard against any Soviet expansion in the Pacific.

Japan has also profited in a straightforward way in Japan also benefited from Korean War. You might be shocked to learn this, but in the end, it's all true. The US control over Japan was crucial in the battle with North Korea since US troops could more efficiently move this way and between Japan as well as North Korea than assuming they were sent by either the US and South Korea, which was under heavy besiegement during the war. This meant that Japan immediately became the principal inventory center of the war effort in Korea. The Japanese economy received a vital boost because of this trade.

Naturally, clearly, the United States can't assume all the glory. Despite the fact the fact that it was US assistance, transactions and stewardship that shook out the Japanese economy in the first place, the Japanese took on a major role in their own swift course of events. Pivotal to their recovery was the reorganization of companies that were previously part of the military-modern complex of Japan, which is now transferring to the private sector.

area. In the same vein, companies such as Mitsubishi who had just made military aircraft and cars, suddenly began to produce them.

Japan has also been the first to dominate the hardware market nearly immediately, and channeled a massive amount of cash, time in addition to energy, into this industry. Due to this focus on commercialization Japan was the second-largest economy in the world during the 1960s, and wouldn't even begin to show signs of decline until late in 1989.

Incredibly, it was during the years 1989-1990, when it became clear that the Cold War started to defrost and Japan's rapid rise started to slow. Japan was able to recover, but it was unable to experience the emotional turmoil it experienced during the post-WWII and Cold War years. However, throughout the Cold War, Japan filled in as the West's guardian and remained an entrepreneur's rampart that slowed the rise of socialism in East Asia.

Chapter 3: Fight Space With Soviets In The Fight For Supremacy In Space

"We have found a way to go into the Moon. It's like the ancient Chinese mainlanders trying to figure out how to reach Formosa; Formosa is the Moon. When we settle on it, our bounce from there to Mars in a similar manner to they did closer to Philippines. Additionally, from this point we travel across the globe. If Austronesians are able to travel in their boats and then disperse to settle in settlements across Oceania We can also utilize our spacecraft and dissolve and settle over all of Milky Way. It could take a lot more time than it did for the Austronesians, but should they have done it, we can too as they are ours."

- Neil Armstrong

Following the demise of the Soviet Union's hardline dictator Joseph Stalin, Nikita Khrushchev became the new Soviet leader. The Khrushchev's residence was marked by saber-shaking as well as suggestions of harmony. Khrushchev would also oversee an era of mechanical progress within the Soviet Union that would have the Russians in the middle of with the Space Race with the United States. It was the Space Race was a rivalry between two powerful powerhouses of the world that had one majority rule and one socialist, to determine who would rule the realm of space exploration.

Khrushchev quickly came out to denounce the wrongdoings committed by Joseph Stalin, who had inexplicably detained, tortured and killed a multitude of Soviets. At a closed session at the Soviet Congress on February 25th in 1956 Khrushchev announced about his displeasure. He said, "It is here that Stalin demonstrated in a whole sequence of instances his insularity as well as his ruthlessness and poor treatment of the power.

He often chose the route of restraint as well as actual destruction, in the face of genuine enemies but also against people who did not carry any offense against the Communist Party or the Soviet Government."

Still waiting in the air to change the course with regard to Soviet history and the vast majority of his fellow Soviets were ready. There were a few events in opposition to Khrushchev in Stalin's hometown Georgia however, the majority were able to go with the same way. Khrushchev really needed to show that the Soviet structure was superior over that of the American one, but the Soviet leader would prefer not to fight World War Three to present his position. He was sure he would discover another avenue. It was not long before he was introduced to science and explored the possibility of room research. In actuality about space, Space Age had begun. Space Age had started during World

War II when the Germans sent a V-2 missile into the skies of the world. The rocket was in use to fight at that moment; indeed it was the world's initial long-range rocket. When it reemerged it exploded into military centers in Britain. Whatever the reasons to the contrary of it was believed that the V-2 was the most manufactured by humans to go out of the earth's atmosphere.

The Germans were the most renowned forerunners in the early days of rocketry, and it was through the Germans who both United States and the Soviet Union obtained a lot of their first equipment. Indeed, prior to even the Space Race even started, there was a second race, where both nations tried to obtain as much information from the Germans as they could. The American effort in this manner began shortly after the war. This was codenamed Operation Paperclip. The efforts to collect the top of German specialization and labor force actually occurred from 1945 until 1959.

The Soviets had their own version of Operation Paperclip, which they called Operation Osoaviakhim. The term "Osoaviakhim" was in fact an abbreviation meaning an Soviet military organization for knowledge. The Soviet efforts to develop German skills were significantly more ferocious than their American partners. In some instances, Germans were persuasively seized. In the book, the German creator, Fritz Karl, depicted his participation in a conference that he attended.

Between 12 until 3 AM at night, when everybody was sleeping. They knew exactly where I lived, but more importantly, just a few days before I was arrested the person who came. They had a key, they carried everything up to the loft and the entrance. One translator informed me that, "Get up! You're being put together for work with us in

Russia," and there were around six officers wearing automatic rifles who surrounded me. When I had to go into the bathroom, they glanced at it to make sure that there would never be a way to get out of the incubating. It was a very intimate procedure.

Like Karl's experiences that in the event that you were "assembled" to be a part of Russia in the past, you really did not have much choices regarding the current situation. In the United States' obtaining of the top German researchers was a bit unique. If the Germans weren't actually absconding to the US and were encouraged to do so by securing prestigious posts in America and the US, where they could continue to conduct their research. Additionally they also had the Americans pledged to pardon and never relive any traumatic events that happened a while in the past, like being involved with war crime.

It was the case for the person who could succeed in running the Marshall Space Flight Center for NASA (National Aeronautics and Space Administration) The Dr. Wernher von Braun. Von Braun was sacked by the Americans at the end of the year of 1945, as were several others "trained experts." After being deported into America in the autumn of 1945, von Braun and his partners required to have their shattered base "figured out" by American authorities. Of particular concern was his work record that involved his management of an entire Peenemunde satellite base that was located situated in Western Germany. The base was a place for work that was restricted in fixation camps.

It's still unclear how much blame ought to be attributed to von Braun. He was certainly under stress at the time because the possibility of being executed or thrown out of into a prison should the way he was working didn't conform to Nazi instructions. Wernher Von Braun employed by the Nazi machine of conflict due to the need for it, since his main goal was to use his rockets to explore space.

However, no matter how you try to alter around a person with such a dark background working for US extravagant projects would not be in the best interests of the populace, and therefore must be hidden. Generallyspeaking, Wernher von Braun's remains would be well-secured inside the wardrobe. In 1950, he along with his friends were discretely relocated and moved to the military base of Huntsville, Alabama, where they would spend the next twenty years advancing with his study of rocketry.

For better or more terrible, von Braun would be America's favorite friend to pass the burden of the Soviet Union's booming rocket program. The Soviets did not manage to capture von Braun on account of the Americans but they did get the most important thing they could have that was his right hand Helmut Grottrup. Grottrup had a solid background in physical science and was a key player in the development and development V-2 rocket's "flight control system."

It is crucial to note the fact that nobody forced Grottrup to divulge more information than was required. Grottrup was able to decide to join the Soviets openly. There are reports that he was eager to escape von Braun and strike it out by himself however, whatever the case the battle was merely a matter of coordination. He was married and had children to worry about and would preferred not to move his family out of Germany. The Soviets permitted rocketry researchers working for their organization to stay in and around the German the region. A few people, especially those who were able to see past the blemishes of socialist Russia similar to what they had left Nazi Germany, the more direct route seemed more appealing.

However, the Soviets sold out the German researchers in the end and breach their promise of a drive nearby. In the course of as the Cold War warmed up, German researchers, such as Helmut Grottrup, were transported out to Russia. According to recent newly discovered Soviet archives In the fall of 1946 around 7,000 Germans, including 500 rocket engineers included--were successfully transferred out of Germany into Russia to work in Soviet-controlled facilities. The reason was that Helmut was genuinely angry at this deceit. In a particular moment the dissatisfied Helmut asked the Soviet head of rocket development Dmitry Ustinov to wait until he and his fellow countrymen would be returned. In response, Dmitry offered the wry statement, "When you can zoom around the world with rockets!" This witty joke about his circumstances was not the kind of joke Helmut Grottrup needed to hear. Instead of having the chance to go to his home country, Helmut needed to be employed in the mysterious Russian bureau that was located in Kapustin Yar, which was located near Kazakhstan. Irmgard witnessed the devastation caused by the climate in Kapustin Yar, and wrote in her journal that the "camels were larger than the vehicles."

However, as time passed, despite the difficulties of the distant region, the scientists began to find their own notch, and began to participate with the projects they had been doing in the name of the Russians. As the rocket testing got underway, Irmgard caught the energy being distinct from all the other things and wrote in her diary that it was "very similar to Peenemunde when we conducted the first of our experiments."

The Russians were not as fascinated with the German researchers. They were quick to rid their brains generally, but when Russian researchers were able duplicate everything they were taught by the Germans directed and commanded, the Germans were swiftly eliminated. It wasn't an German researcher who ended into running the Soviet space program, but rather the Ukrainian-born Sergei Korolev. Korolev was involved in the initial Soviet research into rocketry in the 1930s, but his name was snatched up during one of Stalin's notorious purges.

Sergei was smuggled off to into work camps until he finally released in 1944. Following the end of the war, Korolev was on the scene, overseeing the design of German rockets as well as creating his own plans. The Soviets performed their duties to the point that they would not divulge his name, remaining secretive. Sergei Korolev was referred to only in the title of "Boss Engineer."

In essence initially Russian point of view when they were talking about rocketry, in actuality like the American one, didn't have as much of a space trip, in the sense that it was war weapons. The Russians had a lot of space in

Particularly, they were attracted to the idea of creating intercontinental long-range missiles (ICBMs). With the legendary Korolev as their leader in particular, the Soviets could take advantage of the top Americans and directing the initial ICBM dispatch in the year 1957. However, despite developing such impressive combat equipment used by Russia's military Russian army, Korolev was effectively looking for a way to apply his techniques to space exploration.

There was a chance for him to take advantage of it when he read reports that America was considering putting the satellite in space. Korolev looked up Soviet premier Khrushchev and told him about the events and his fear about the Soviets were getting behind. In order to not be overshadowed, Khrushchev allowed Korolev to depart on a satellite mission. Following approval, Korolev went max speed into a design task which would lead to the launch the development of Sputnik 1, the world's first satellite to circle in 1957.

The possibility that satellites orbit Earth is a common occurrence of everyday life. However, back in the day the thought that Russians had a device that could directly fly over America, but from space -- was alarming. Americans were waiting for a long time to get a response. It was due to the small satellite dubbed Sputnik which Sputnik was the reason that Space Race started decisively. Incredulous of the circling object Von Braun's control group from the United States had him race to improve the American design, known as Explorer 1.

the satellite was swiftly launched in January of the year 1958 in order to demonstrate to that the Soviet Union that America could take on them in a circle. In the month of January, 1959 the Soviets decided to increase the bar by sending satellites which was circling Earth and also was released from the gravity of Earth out and out again to turn around the sun. In late spring 1959 Wernher von Braun and his American overseers , at that point, took the initiative to step up and launched Explorer 6, which would enjoy the privilege of taking the first ever photograph of Earth from space.

It is evident that the conflict to room firsts seemed becoming to full blast at this time. One success from one end was followed by another on the other side. In addition, before the year had even started out it was discovered that the Russians sent an art work to the Moon (it was actually directly with it) and was followed by another that was launched by taking pictures of the moon's other side. With these rapid achievements that the US was feeling as if it was left behind. For the elite members of that United States military, the accomplishment gap was not just a damper for space exploration however, it also brought the public with a serious threat to security. You may laugh about it today, but there was a real fear during the time of the accomplishment hole that

Russians could set up an operational station at the Moon and then use it to unleash attacks on Earth and in particular the US. In the midst of these thoughts of dread, when John F. Kennedy vowed to send Americans to the Moon before the decade was over, von Braun and his similar German researchers were formally transferred to the top of the recently established National Aeronautics and Space Administration (NASA) in the year 1960. In the beginning, the agency was focused on NASA's Marshall Space Flight Center in Huntsville, Alabama. There, they were given an "order" to develop the launch of a rocket with the possibility of taking American space travellers towards the Moon. Soon after the launch, von Braun was made the "boss of the planner" of what would eventually be"the Saturn V rocket. Wernher von Braun employed an additional former Nazi, Arthur Rudolph, who worked alongside him to Germany as a chief of tasks of the rocket V-2. The Saturn V idea kept on evolving and being developed, it was not set in stone that it would need an entirely different dispatch system.

and this is the reason why for this reason, land was bought for this reason in Florida. Cape Canaveral, situated on the eastern part of Florida was selected as the site of dispatch for future models. To serve as a storage facility for the massive Saturn V, the Vertical Assembly Building was constructed on the tiny Merritt Island, arranged simply in the middle of Florida. This massive stockroom was designed by a different German rocket engineer and friend with von Braun, Bernhard Tessmann.

But, even as the plans were being developed however, the Soviets actually had the upper hand in the race, and they kept pace with it in an impressive way in the month of April, 1961, when they sent Gagarin, the most famous of men, into space. This was especially troubling for the newly elected American presidential candidate, John F. Kennedy who had run for the presidency on a stage where he announced that he would finally "close the gap" during space. Space Race. The announcement was not an official statement, unlike any other moment in recent history to get one man to the Moon and do this prior to that of the Soviet Union.

In the meantime they were doing to make up for their lost time. After Gagarin successfully circled Earth, NASA sent American space traveler Alan Shepard up into space on May 5th of 1961. It is important to note this Shepard was the most prominent American to orbit the earth, but He wasn't the first American who circled Earth. This honor is shared in the same category as John Glenn, who surrounded Earth with a circle during the month of February in 1962.

At this moment at this point, the American NASA was making several steps that were relatively quick however, they had an extremely difficult but not impossible job ahead, assuming that they had to take on the Soviets.

To realize Kennedy's dream of landing being the first man to walk on the Moon prior to the

In the decade that was over, NASA got a huge infusion of funds from the central government in the period between the years 1961 to 1964. NASA had some major advancements during this time but misfortune struck in the year 1967, when three group members--Gus Grissom Ed White, and Roger Chaffee--kicked the bucket with an explosive blast while testing to test a piece of equipment. NASA was both dejected and embarrassed by the incident and the Soviets were quick to hail it as moment as another indication that Americans had fallen behind badly when it came to this Space Race.

In spite of it being true it was true that America had been open to and threatening in any incident that could come to them however, the Soviets maintained a tight lid on their mishaps so everyone else would not be able to see the incident. For instance, Russian cosmonaut Vladimir Komarov hit Earth on the 24th of April in 1967. The specialization he was on--Soyuz 1 --is believed to have been smacked by numerous special problems. The power of the specialty's electrical system was slowed when a sun charged charger failed and the wires that were receiving it were not able to function properly.

send, interfering with the route, interfering with. Despite these issues, Komarov was a gifted enough pilot to get through these difficulties and guide the craft back to Earth's climate to reemerge. The final flaw of this poorly planned specialty was the moment when the boat's arrival parachutes failed to transmit properly and made the spacecraft crash into the outermost layer of earth. In the end, all that was left of the cosmonaut's bound to earth were ashes and bones that had been roasted.

According to the official account, this sudden change is the end to the tale. But there is a fear in the form of a theory, that is available for a number of years to this day and suggests that there's some other aspect to this account. This theory suggests it. Vladimir Komarov realized that he was not happy from the beginning He realized that the creation of his art was recklessly taken for granted.

Chief Designer Korolev had died in the previous year, and a number of Soviet projects were more streamlined and speeded along by Korolev's less attentive successors. In the event that Komarov was aware that the work was not perfect, he believed he was in a position to refuse. The situation was depicted in the book Starman by Jamie Doran and Piers Bizony in 2011 , in the book Starman. The book after that, makes the more harrowing case that American intelligence agents stationed in Turkey were able to receive a recording of Komarov's last remarks in the direction of Russian command and control. Komarov was clearly "crying in fury," reviling the bungled work that Soviet specialists had completed on his work. As things are as they are what was the supposed source of this vast array of striking subtleties? According to

In the book, it was the work of a former KGB employee identified as Venyamin Russayev whose name hasn't been verified.

Conspiracy theories, including speculations about Soviet programs in space (and surprisingly the American one) are the exact same thing. For quite a long time to this point it seems that it seems that the "Lost Cosmonauts" theory has been popularized. The theory states that a small number of astronauts were carried before Yuri Gagarin. They threw the bucket, and are still circling Earth or were hurled out into deep space.

Although this could be for fans of sci-fi the book will stick to the facts of. As it stands what we really know about the tragic trip of Vladimir Komarov is that his parachutes fell apart, his art was crushed into the ground, and he perished in the blaze.

In any case however, the Soviets continued to pursue their quest for strength, and then they intensified their pursuit of the Moon as a result of Komarov's loss. The year 1968 was when they sent Zond 5, a mechanical artifact that carried no humans but rather a handful of turtles, and sent them circling all around Moon. Although it's not as thrilling as human flight but it was an additional first which could be attributed in the hands of the Soviets. It was the first time where any life form from Earth were sent into the lunar orbit and safely returned home. Apart from the deliberate publicity win this mission revealed little more than what the Soviets already knew. The most important information gathered were about the effects of radiation on Earth's life. In addition to being gluttonous the turtles were not affected by space travel. But even in their ability to had to endure another trip to Earth the brave turtles would not live much longer. They were subsequently dismantled by Soviet scientists, who wanted to study the effects from space upon their bodies.

Meanwhile, NASA, not having any intention of being abandoned once again chose to beat the Soviets. Before reaching the possible limit, the US created a lasting impression on the globe by sending turtles but individuals to circle around the Moon in Apollo 8. Kennedy's proposal for sending Americans to the outermost level of Too much before the decade's closing was within reach.

The Soviets seem to be about to of now be settling for rout once it came to the race towards the Moon suddenly changed gears. Instead of focusing their attention on the Moon however, they made a remarkable first in another field , with the first docking of two mades and the primary exchange of team members between two made docked. These are two significant accomplishments and will be crucial for the subsequent activities of room stations where artworks are expected to be able to

It is safe to dock safely at the station.

However, despite these triumphs of Soviet technology, NASA would take all the excitement by eventually placing the first people on the outermost layer of the Moon during 1969. The whole world was in awe as the first humans were able to step out into the world for the very first time. It was the final astonishing conclusion of the Space Race. There was not a single shot fired however America was believed to have won the space race.

Chapter 4: How Cold War Calculus Affected The Middle East

"Israel is the only nation in which everyone is supportive of American the United States, with resistance and cooperation are one. In addition, I speak to all population of Israel who say, "Thanks, America.' And we're a partner of America and we're among the principal reliable partner for America within the Middle East."

- Benjamin Netanyahu

Though you might not be aware of that on the off chance that you turned on the news that you normally see, it in a certain degree at the time of writing and by all accounts, is not reporting one of the most important news of 2020 that is the agreement for harmony between Israel and Bahrain, UAE (United Arab Emirates) and Bahrain. Both of these Arab Gulf State nations had been enemies of Israel from the time of its creation in 1948. Similar to other countries in the Middle East at that point as well, both UAE and Bahrain were in a position of threat towards Israel.

Israel's birth, although not directly linked to the competing philosophies in during the Cold War, immediately turned into a major focus in the war among both Cold War powers. The Soviets wanted to capitalize on Arab dislike of the work of Israel to benefit in managing the West. Although even though the Middle East players might not be socialists at first but they, too could have played one superpower against the other.

To discover what Cold War analytics meant for the Middle East, one first needs to know the way in which the cutting-edge province of Israel came into being. The full story of the area is beyond the scope of this publication, so this is going to be as short as is possible.

The Jewish argument to Israel goes back to the time of the Bible approximately 1000 years prior to Christ. After that you can fast forward to the time of Jesusabout 30 CE. Israel was crucial to during the Roman Empire. Jews were actually living in the country, yet an absolute control remained in the hands of Roman representative in charge. This was not a pleasant relationship and the situation got to a point of no return during the Bar Kokhba Revolt of 132 CE. It was a major uprising in the face of Roman power, and Jewish innovator Bar Kokhba raised up a crowd of 200,000 people to challenge Rome's military power.

The consequences of Bar Kokhba, his supporters as well as all of the inhabitants of Israel were not good. All of the men under Bar Kokhba's leadership were either executed or taken away for Rome with chains. All in all around a substantial part of one million Jews were executed, and the

The survivors were exiled the survivors were exiled from Jerusalem. Roman The Emperor Hadrian was so irritated with the resistance that he sought to discover the entirety from Judaism from the region. Hadrian did not allow the Jewish training from receiving the Torah and had to ban Jewish customs. In an effort to in a true sense sever Israel from the Torah, Hadrian then, at this point, named the territory "Syria Palaestina" which later became known as "Palestine."

Then, you can continue to move ahead towards 325 CE. It was the year that Roman Emperor Constantine was the head of the Council of

Nicaea, and began creating laws that were favorable for Christianity. In the past, prior to Constantine, Christians were regularly assaulted, but following Constantine was elected, they flourished. Christians then began to moved into Palestine and Israel, constructed temples and Christianized the region, viewing it as the country that Christ was once in.

Christian dominance in Israel/Palestine continued through until the 7th century, when the Persians gained control of the region. The Persian occupation proved to be only for a short time, after they were pushed out in the year 625. But, Roman Christians wouldn't have many days to celebrate as another incredible power known as Islam was able to ascend in Arabia and attacked the region in the 630s and later. Israel/Palestine finally fell to the mighty power of Islam and remained in Muslim control until the moment that marked the First Crusade in the last decade in the decade 1090. Crusaders would remain within their respective parts of the Holy Land until they were finally exiled by Islamic power about 200 years later in the 1290s. The land that is Israel/Palestine was then governed by a small number of Muslim pioneers, before at finally being joined under the Islamic power to be reckoned with by the Ottoman Empire in 1516. The Ottomans will then govern the territory until around 1918, the year at which it was that the Ottoman Empire was crushed in World War I. The Ottomans were on the wrong aspect of the war by following those of the Central Powers of Germany, Austria-Hungary and Bulgaria. Following their fall to the Central Powers, the British assumed the control of Palestine. England then in 1922, issued a decree in which they pledged to create "an unavoidable nation to Jews within Palestine." According to reports, when the order was ratified in 1922, around 58,000 Jews were actually living in the region. But, by the time the end of the decade the number of Jews began to grow quickly. As Jewish movements grew stronger, so also, did the nearby Arab dislike. In spite of the customary Jewish tradition dating back to the millennia ago, the present inhabitants did not see any Jewish issue with the land. There were massive protests and uprisings orchestrated by Arab pioneers in opposition to the Jews.

However, the movement continued as did demands for Britain to be viewed as that it was a Jewish state. England was adamant about escalating pressures in the region further, pondered whether or not it should decide to do this.

It wasn't until after the end of Second World War that an American-backed plan seemed to finally establish an actual Jewish state. The plan was based on the detestations caused by the Holocaust that was a large part of the plan was still in the air plans to collaborate with a nation that was a place for Jews. When the issue was brought before the United Nations, even the Soviet Union supported an arrangement to partition Palestine into an official Jewish state. The majority of people believed that the Jews were entitled to a security for themselves due to having suffered so much suffering and suffering imposed on them during the conflict.

Oviet ambassador Andrei Gromyko likely summarized this opinion in the best way in the United Nations.

As we're likely aware, the desires of a large portion of the Jewish population are entwined with the question of Palestine and its future structure. This is a fact that doesn't require confirmation. In the conflict of the past in the past, the Jewish public was in great despair and was left in a state of. It is clear that the United Nations can't and should not accept the current circumstances by ignoring it, as this is in contradiction to the high standards set forth within its Charter. The fact that none of the Western European state has had the opportunity to ensure the protection of the basic rights that are enjoyed by the Jewish public and to defend it from the brutality of fundamentalist murderers reveals the desire that the Jewish to create an independent state. It is unjust to contemplate this, and not to recognize the rights to people in the Jewish public to comprehend this dream. However, this kind of empathy was not shared by Israel's Arab neighbors. And when Israel was declared a nation on May 14 1948, a brutal and swift war was launched against the country. In actual fact, Israel had just been officially recognized as a nation just one day, and was fighting off an increase from a handful of Arab nations in the same moment. Israel

It was ready, and stunned the world by standing up to the attack and taking steps forward. The threats ended in a ceasefire at the end of March of 1949, however Israel's enemies would never consider Israel as a genuine state.

In their anger and rage over the statehood of Israel that a number of Arab powerhouses began to look towards the Soviet Union for help. Initially the Soviets believed that they could affect the ways of approaching Israel but after they realized that this was not possible the Soviets began to look to the Arabs regardless. They first went to the Arab

One of the nations which the Soviets were looking for one of which was Egypt. The rise from Egyptian the pioneer Gamal Abdel Nasser who was a fervent opponent of colonialists was met with a favourable reception by the Soviets.

In 1955, the Russians had been supplying armies to Egypt. Particularly, after Nasser made the decision to nationalize Suez Canal, he was brought up to the highest level feasible to the Soviets. In the Suez Canal was underlying the 19th century by the British at the time that Egypt was still under British the rule of pioneers. Following Egypt was liberated away from British, Egyptian patriots started to

The Suez Canal was in need of nationalization. Suez Canal, which was at the same time being managed through both British as well as the French. The situation reached a tipping point in 1956, when Gamal Abdel Nasser took on this.

This led to the joint attacks of Britain and France in an attempt to prevent entry into the trench. This was an invasion which was quelled by an Israeli incursion to the Sinai. These actions would have repercussions globally in the event that the Soviets engaged to defend in their Egyptian customers state. In the end, the Soviet Union undermined military activity and also a surprising nuclear trade in the possibility that the belligerents failed to quit Egypt in peace. This led to for the United States to show up and ask each of the belligerents to be evacuated from Egypt immediately.

US president Eisenhower was concerned about the likelihood that the situation in Egypt could lead to the outbreak as well as out World War Three, and He was not prepared to allow such a thing to happen under his supervision, specifically on this remote area. This was a humiliating hit to British preeminence in particular (it was believed that British expertise had been in place been in place for a long time, and had passed) however the two countries Britain and France protested and retreated their troops.

Israel and, later did not quit the Sinai until the year 1957. Then they would return, with the final departure from the area just shortly after that EgyptIsrael Peace Treaty of 1979. The way in which the Soviets stood up so strongly for Egypt and clearly scared Americans United States enough to get them to force the aggressors to leave in a major and deliberate publicity win in the name of Soviet Russia.

The Soviets who had enjoyed some significant victory in this particular political battle used this to show themselves as heroes of the longshot , and the people who defended the less developed countries against the tyranny of power. For the Soviets this was the second time the West was at its peak. Due to the obvious risk of Soviet counters The United States was persuaded to gain control over its allies.

However, to claim that Soviet influence led to the US look squinty is an untrue description, as it would be assumed as if America was opposed to the invasion of Egypt regardless. Eisenhower's British, French, and Israeli allies had generally resisted any form of authority and had directed an action without his consent. This way there was no large amount the time that the Eisenhower group was a bit squinting, in the sense that they followed through with their plans to get their partners back to normal.

Contrary to that of the Cuban Missile Crisis of the 1960s, when the Soviets generally changed their course in the face of American tension The Suez Crisis was not of American plans. All things being equal, America was basically maneuvered into the conflict. However the reality of things and the way in which it is perceived are often two different aspects. In addition, when it came into what was known as the Cold War math of the Middle East, discernment was all that was needed.

Chapter 5: Cuba, Vietnam, And Growing Social

Unrest

"Traditionalists frequently depict Marx as well as Lenin as scholars not ever pondering that their visions inspired Russia and China, the two nations who were urged to build a world that takes into consideration human endurance, assuming that the that the government does not immediately release the crook and end the war."

- Fidel Castro

While the Eisenhower organization was coming to a conclusions in the final period of the 1950s, an astonishing place of convergence of that Cold War was starting to emerge just ninety miles away from the Florida coast in a secret location known as Cuba. In earlier years, Cuba had been controlled by Americanaccommodating autocracies, the most recent of which was helmed by a person named Fulgencio Batista. Batista's system suddenly came to an end when a radical by his name Fidel Castro came up with a plan to stage an uprising.

It was the American CIA (Central Intelligence Agency) was aware that Batista's days were past but they didn't have an extreme group of progressives to rule. Therefore, all things considered they attempted to create an alternative to another leader with the hope that a new appearance would calm the rage from Cubans. Cuban public. The Americans stood by Cuban general Eulogio Cantillo who signed an armistice and announced that Batista was going to leave the throne. Cantillo made the Cuban people know that Batista was likely to be arrested but in reality the latter was granted a secure sections of Cuba and left on the 31st of December in 1958.

the next day the next day, the next day, General Cantillo acting as a kingmaker, asked an earlier Supreme Court judge by the name of Carlos Piedra to step in as the head of a temporary government until a real political contest could take place. But, assuming that the Pentagon believed that Cuban Progressives would remain satisfied with the new plan, they ended up getting confused. Castro and his comrades weren't overly pleased with these events which is why they travel to Havana --the capital city of Cuba--to work it out for themselves.

After arriving in the capital city, Castro and his associates gathered together General Cantillo who was taken to prison (he was released within a few years of the fact, and then escaped to Florida) Then, they took over the real power. The moment they arrived, Fidel Castro attempted to eliminate himself from socialism. In the time he traveled to in the United States in 1959, the Cuban remained adamant in any aspect of the socialist ideology. Fidel Castro

Expected to have a meeting the American President Eisenhower at the time of his visit however, he ended into securing the vice presidency Richard Nixon all things being the same. Castro and Nixon seemed to have a problem with one another from the beginning. Nixon did not accept communism for a short time.

Following their meeting, Nixon innocent with regards to socialism or was under socialism's discipline. My guess is the former." Following the time that Castro returned to Cuba and the relationship among both the United States and the new Cuban government continued to be highlighted. When a young representative from Massachusetts under the name of John F. Kennedy was selected to succeed Eisenhower after the death of Eisenhower, the correspondence between US and Cuba had ended.

Kennedy was able to complete his mission with the promise that he would be able to improve the situation in Cuba. He was now required to put his money in the right place. In order to avoid the Cold War loss of Cuba falling into socialism, Kennedy put together a group of Cuban exiles attempting to cooperate to eliminate Cuba from the Castro system. The efforts would be brought full circle after 1961, when the Bay of Pigs disaster in 1961. The name for the event stemmed from the location the point at which these agents came in at, which was in relation to Cuba also known as"the "Cove of Pigs."

In a bid to prevent the possibility of Cold War a conflict, Kennedy made an effort to keep the operation strictly Cuban issue, with only Cuban soldiers included. In the end, the event ended in a terribly disappointing failure and the entire group of Cuban exiles were executed or captured. The US had previously portrayed Castro as an ideologue from the socialist party in the aftermath of the Bay of Pigs was over, he was a riot and Castro was not influenced by

They would claim that Castro "was extremely well-understood. Castro made a public appearance and declared that Castro was a Marxist following the disastrous bay of Pigs invasion.

Castro was at present captivated to the Soviets and had become the most prominent player of the Cold War. With Kennedy's gang frantically plotting to take over the system, Castro requested the Soviets to help. He probably expected to be given conventional arms, but to his shock they suggested that the Soviets suggested that atomic missiles be placed on the island to serve as to deter.

Soviet Prime Minister Nikita Khrushchev was meanwhile working on his ability to exert pressure to his country US in Suez Crisis. Suez Crisis from quite a time and thought that it was time for him to try his hand again. Khrushchev admitted the fact that Kennedy wasn't a kin to Eisenhower and believed that Eisenhower was a simple man to

To be a jerk, Khrushchev more likely than had thought that tampering with Kennedy could be just only a drop in the bucket. However, he was muddled upand Kennedy would prove to the Soviets precisely what his motives were. After U-2 government operative plane images confirmed that Cuba had nuclear rockets, Kennedy took his interests into the public eye. Live on television and on the internet, he revealed all the globe about what Soviets did. At the point of his speech and in the process of making his own to be understood. Kennedy declared that if the atomic bomb was launched from Cuba and hit the US, the US would find the Soviets accountable and unleash America's nuclear weapons on and within the Soviet Union itself. The Soviet Union would be Khrushchev this time who was the one to "blink." In order to avoid a nuclear conflict with Cuba, Khrushchev promptly contacted Kennedy to let him off. On the other hand, Kennedy consented to eliminate some nuclear weapons that were buried in Turkey in exchange for the Soviets taking away the nuclear weapons from Cuba. To calm Cuba, Khrushchev even figured out how to secure an agreement from Kennedy to stop any effort to overthrow the Castro regime. There would not be any more nukes on Cuban territory, however, there would also be no any Bay of Pigs-style attack for Castro to fret about.

It was a good idea to have a happy host for any gathering, however Castro was left feeling irritated and slighted. He was particularly upset by the fact that his country US along with the USSR agreed to this agreement without even speaking to Castro in any way. Fidel also criticized Khrushchev for being "frail" in his trade between the Americans. Castro believed his fellow Americans had been able to win this particular round of Cold War excessively easily.

However, another colossal test during this Cold War was warming up at this time around Vietnam and this one could not be as easily completed. Vietnam was experiencing huge social unrest from the time of the World War. Prior to World War II, Vietnam was an independent French state. After France was sucked into Nazi Germany in

World War II, France tracked down some of its earlier frontiers in difficult conditions.

After surrendering to the Nazis and the Nazis, after the Nazis surrendered, French Vichy government took take over. It was a supporter of Hitler and under the rules of the new alliance, Vichy France would be allowed to remain and keep in line with its states. Germany's ally to the Axis, Japan, had different plans. As the Japanese began to spread across East Asia, overcoming a one area after another at a time, the Japanese began to descend to Vichy France to give

These regional concessions.

In the end, Japan eventually decided to retain control over French Vietnam for its own reasons, Hitler deliberately ignored and allowed the Japanese to go on with their dispute, showing the kind of arrangement Hitler could turn out to be. Japan let the French to finish a small portion of their prior managerial duties in managing the area but with Japanese soldiers all over the place it was clear who was in charge. Locally, a group consisting of Vietnamese warriors, comprised of socialists from the neighborhood, known as"the

Viet Minh, ascended and began to engage in close-quarters battle with the Japanese.

It is believed that the United States really upheld the Viet Minh, especially as they were a partner in the war against Japan. However, when Japan was defeated following World War II found some solution, there was a poop when the French tried to assert their authority over Vietnam. It was the socialist Viet Minh, who had tried to get rid of the possessions of Japanese soldiers, were not going to surrender to French domain. They needed to be independent. It was the United States, which was generally opposed to provinces at this point (the US had constrained Britain to give up a few of their own after the war) and also for autonomous nations based on voting were at first supportive of their former wartime partner and in the Viet Minh. However, when it became clear that the Cold War grabbed hold, US authorities realized it was the Viet Minh was required to transform Vietnam into a strict socialist state. The Americans were dismayed , and they began helping the French. France did not end up as a social-democratic counterpart, in any event and eventually pulled out of Vietnam completely.

Similar to what was the case similarly to the situation in Germany as well as similar to what had happened in Germany and the Korean Peninsula, Vietnam was separated into two states in 1954: socialist North and the majority-rule industrialist South. At the Geneva Conference that followed the French withdrawal The Soviets actually required Vietnam's Vietnamese socialists to recognize the possibility of a separate segment, arguing that it would provide them with an the opportunity to balance and increase their power.

However, it wasn't long when the North began to turn towards the South and began to engage to ensure the complete dominance of Vietnam. This was an appropriate infringement in an United States strategy of regulation in the same way as it was the case in Korea in the past, the US was forced to intervene. The US could not swiftly deploy troops to the area initially, but it was the United States essentially provided weapons and other items to those in the South Vietnamese, trusting that this additional aid was enough to defeat North Vietnam on their own.

However, when the South was beginning to falling by the middle of the 1960s and it was at this point that the United States concluded the time was right to make a decision. Then, in February of 1965 US president Lyndon B. Johnson authorized a bombing operation that was later referred to in the form of Operation Rolling Thunder. In the same year, the socialist China sent experts to help strengthen security forces within North Vietnam, making underlying repairs to railway lines and the rest of the frameworks, which would later become the main targets for Operation Rolling Thunder.

A little less than a month from the time Operation Rolling Thunder initiated, the majority of US combat troops entered South Vietnam. They were asked to guard US air bases in the region. In the spring of 1965, the amount of US soldiers in Vietnam was expected to grow to over 100,000. In the meantime, China would wind up creating a large amount of Chinese soldiers, who were tucked in among the Vietnamese competitors, in Vietnam throughout the next few years.

While this was an utter increase in the conflict however, this was a time when the United States actually needed to take its time to avoid launching itself into a frenzied battle against China as well as with the Soviet Union. The Soviets in the sense that they could maintained their compass towards North Vietnam genuinely attentive, however, as the conflict grew as did their support. Their assistance grew significantly following Leonid Brezhnev, not set in stone to make it easier to make use of the Soviet Union's military power, replaced the sham Nikita Khrushchev who had lost a lot of his trustworthiness with his fellow Soviets following the Cuban Missile Crisis. In 1965 the Soviets signed a peace agreement together with North Vietnamese, which would provide a financial guide along with military equipment as well as specialized advice for the Vietnamese socialists fight. The Soviets were currently coming out of the darkness with their assistance. In the event there was any confusion and chaos, they made a public statement. Soviet Union gave a public declaration that read:

The Democratic Republic of Vietnam (DRV) which is the Communist camp located in the south-east of Asia has taken on an important role in the fight against the American government and has made its commitment to the preservation of peace in Asia and across the world. The governments that comprise and of the USSR along with DRV have examined the circumstances. Both countries unreservedly denounce the repressive actions of the United States, and particularly the savage attacks of American aircraft on the domain of DRV. The USSR will not be unaffected by providing security to a friendlier communist country and will offer the DRV crucial guidance and support.

It was clear to everyone that the Soviets believed it was their duty to safeguard the country's youth that was socialist. Before the decade ended it was reported that approximately 3/4 of the guides given towards North Vietnam North Vietnamese was from the Soviets. However there was a chance that it was clear that the Soviet Union was going to confront a challenge. It wasn't China's assistance of Vietnam that caused the problem and not China's involvement in the region of Vietnam.

As both Soviets as well as China Chinese had socialist inclinations, it is likely that they'd be partners in common. But by the final part into the

50s both socialist juggernauts began to move into distinct bearings. From then on they would compete rather than collaborate. In 1968, the tensions were reaching a dangerous high point which led to Soviet fighters advancing along the Chinese border.

The strains would explode into the air in 1969 in a line battle which would result in more than 200 people dead. Although that the Soviet Union and China never officially fought in this way, the brutal assault was about as close as one can get without even thinking about the possibility of it happening. As volatile as relations between China and the Soviet Union were, at the time in the Vietnam War the two sides came to a point in the sense that Vietnam had to decide on whether it should receive the majority of its aid through China or from the Soviets and/or from Chinese.

Given that the Soviets would have a lot to gain from equip themselves with military equipment at the time it was quite simple of a decision to make. As the political inclination of the Vietnamese was made recognized, Mao Zedong started to reduce support, and also had Chinese soldiers begin making their departure. At this point, Vietnam seemed to have an "perpetual waterway" of resources and provisions flowing in out of to the Soviet Union.

Therefore, the likelihood that America might actually win this bloodbath began to be called into debate. Even before the military's control centers would admit that their position that Vietnam War was not working and that it was not working, the American people were aware. There was a growing discontent on the roadways as a result of the war. There were sporadic combats against the conflict in the 1960s and into the early 1970s However, it wasn't until following the Tet Offensive, which occurred in 1968 that fighting in the home really began to gain momentum.

The Tet Offensive was a significant offensive led by North Vietnamese that took the conflict to more than 100 different locations in South Vietnam. This massive offensive was designed to erode American confidence and compel the South

Vietnamese to desert. The North Vietnamese were fruitful in these areas. American soldiers were at the end prepared to confront North Vietnamese. North Vietnamese, however when these events were reported to the American people through the media, many Americans began to question the likelihood that an United States truly beating the North Vietnamese.

It seemed that no matter what number of Vietnamese who escaped the ring during these unrelenting assaults They would just continue to send more, causing an endless impasse that was bleeding. In reality, as a newsman Walter Cronkite voiced that equivalent sentiment when he remarked on media coverage that it appeared "more certain than any other moment in recent history that the terrible experience of Vietnam will come to an be a stalemate." This caused the President Lyndon B. Johnson to publicly grieve, "Assuming I've lost Cronkite it's my loss to Middle America."

And Johnson appeared to be firmly in his judgment of the events, as it was this recognition in that Vietnam was a war that seemed to last forever that could lead those who were not opposed to the war from a philosophical standpoint to view that the entire process an ineffective act. After such a rapid reduction in confidence in the war fighting became something that was routine. With these developments the confused LBJ would not be looking for an election in 1968, instead deciding to pass on the idea of a different official candidate to other Democrats.

in the lead leading up to the 1968 presidential race ahead of the rest until the 1968 election, ahead of the rest until the 1968 election, the United States would turn into an enraged hotspot of social unrest. There were wars about and the Vietnam War as well as massive rumblings and fights about social equality. The leader of modern social equality movement the reverend Martin Luther King Jr. was killed on April 4th of 1968. His death was greeted with grief.

Agony and outrage anger and pain, and a number of American urban communities were engulfed in the flames.

In the meantime in the meantime, in the meantime, Democratic Party was attempting to determine who could take on the presidency in the place of LBJ. In the spring of 1968 the Democratic leadership included the Senator Eugene McCarthy, Senator George McGovern and senator Robert F. Kennedy, and LBJ's vice president, Hubert Humphrey. In a similar field the former VP usually has the highest influence and if they decide to run typically replace the President they were under.

However, Hubert Humphrey was facing Robert F. Kennedy in the primary elections and Kennedy was extremely well-known. In 1963, the American public was deeply disappointed when Robert's brother President John F. Kennedy, was shot dead in 1963. They could sense the dead previous president's passion and

Goals in Robert Kennedy as well as many who were confident that Robert might be able to reestablish some aspects of John F. Kennedy's legendary Camelot time in Washington had been deprived of.

When Robert Kennedy won the California essential in 1968, he seemed to be in a position to beat Humphrey and the other contenders for the task. Tragically, Robert's story was ended by the professional killer's slug shortly after he won his California essential. After being shot at distance by a single shooter and a Palestinian extremist identified as Sirhan Bizar Sirhan, Kennedy was hurried to an emergency clinic. Kennedy would die the next day. The crushing blow he dealt in the midst of a presidential race was devastating.

As a quick result of Kennedy's death, some openly considered whether the Soviets might have in one way or other been involved. Following discussions of the professional murderer did not reveal any links to the Kremlin All things considered it revealed the thoughts of a man who was extremely disturbed. In fact, he was so upset to the point where it was his intention to make the terrifying claim that the killer "passed off" and was not aware of shooting Kennedy in spite of the fact that a plethora of people saw him perform it. Sirhan did not initially offer an explanation for the attack at first, but during a discussion during 1989, the man stated that he was angry with Robert Kennedy for his maintained aid to Israel.

Kennedy's death Kennedy determined how to make Hubert Humphrey leading the pack and secured the position. However the commotion caused by Kennedy's death placed the previous Vice-President in a tough spot. When he realized that his opponent in the Republican side was the previous President Eisenhower's powerful Richard

Nixon, Humphrey realized that he was about to embark on an uncomfortable journey. Nixon in reference to the terrible turmoil in the country, portrayed his self in the role of the "peace and lawful" president. He took on the majority of Americans who weren't on the streets dissenting, but trying to get their jobs done and pay the costs of the families they had.

Nixon promised this section of electorate, which called the "quiet majority," that he would take the request until the end of the world. He also stated that he would bring harmony to Vietnam "with honour." The truth would be revealed it was Hubert Humphrey was getting a tiny amount or "help" from an unexpected source. It turned out that the Soviets preferred the chance to have Hubert Humphrey and the Democrats in the Oval Office than a hardline Republican like Nixon.

So as a result, the Russians attempted to broker President Johnson's last attempt to negotiate a cease-fire to North Vietnam. Although it may be,

Russian government actually compelled their socialist allies to fulfill some of the American demands during the negotiations on harmony, believing that it would help the replacement for President Johnson, Hubert Humphrey, enough to allow him to be elected into the presidency. Even though the last decade of time has seen Americans contemplate the implications of Russian intrusions into American races, these kinds of exercises occurred before. They were just another device within the Soviet toolbox in the Cold War.

Nixon In the meanwhile, Nixon time, was living in a complete the fear that Johnson could find a way to an orderly management of Vietnam before the presidential race. Nixon was doing well in the polls, but Nixon emphasized that an extraordinary piece of good fortune for Democrats could be able to figure out how to place Hubert Humphrey on top come the final day of voting. For Nixon it was not a good thing. Nixon was the one who could bring "harmony with respect" into the Cold War disaster, not anyone else. It was a shocking event in October which he could not bear.

For his part, it was fortunate that he did not have to. It was not due to basis of the North Vietnam pulled out of peace talks, but because the leader of beleaguered South Vietnam, President Nguyen

Van Thieu (Nguyen Van Thieu) was able to save his country without delay. Nixon was then was able to went on to win the political race with a flurry of. If we assume that Richard Nixon had a mysterious arrangement to stop this Vietnam War, it wasn't immediately clear during his first term as president.

Ixon's principal procedure was one that was difficult to follow. It included assisting South Vietnamese powers, preparing the South Vietnamese, and supplying them with military equipment, while slowly pulling off US troops. This was the so-called "Vietnamization" strategy that was designed to make those South Vietnamese more associated with the war and less dependent on US troops in the field. It was essentially an overturning of the progress which had been in place over the longer term and the arrangement was not perfect on several levels.

The first and most important thing is that first and foremost, the South Vietnamese, generally, had lost their desire to fight the North quite a while back in the past. In the end they were completely dependent on US military forces which meant that South Vietnam didn't appear to be able to stand in its own hands anytime very soon. However, while Nixon tried to remove troops, he increased the number of bombs and even sent in more troops from neighbouring Cambodia and Laos in an attempt to cause chaos within the line of North Vietnamese.

At this point that Nixon further formulated what he described as "crazy person theory." Nixon required his overseas socialist opponents to believe that he was a crazy person.

The man was clearly distraught and was freaked out. They wanted them to realize that he was insane and stupid and they'd be wary to threaten him in the event this crazy "crazy person" put his fingers on the button and unleashed the rage of nuclear bombs upon them.

It's a bit ridiculous, but Nixon acknowledged that he could fake it and persuade his adversaries to acceptance. Nixon described this to the chief of staff H. R. Haldeman (Nixon was merely calling his name Bob).

Think about it as think about it as the Madman Theory, Bob. I'm requiring to convince the North Vietnamese to accept I've reached a point where I can effectively stop the war. We'll simply say to them that "for the sake of God You realize that Nixon is obsessed with socialism. We cannot restrain him when he's mad--and Nixon is holding the nuclear button" as well Ho Chi Minh himself will be in Paris within two days, begging for peace.

Nixon attempted to terrorize the Soviet Union by this method in 1969, by opposing Cold War shows and participating in a risky, forceful exercise using atomic equipped planes that ran along the Soviet border. Nixon did this with the hope that he could force the Soviets to alter their policy regarding North Vietnam. In addition, despite the fact that these actions could convince the Soviets to enter to arms control agreements in the near future but it was to the extent of little to contribute to the search to achieve peace in Vietnam.

The conflict would drag throughout Nixon's first term and through his second. In the meantime there was a time when it was discovered that the North Vietnamese had extended their hatred to the locals of Cambodia. This made the situation less secure than it actually could be, Nixon fought back by sending a combined force comprised of

Americans as well as South Vietnamese into Cambodia in April of 1970. This escalation of the conflict caused the shock of Americans and South Vietnamese, and then fights regularly took place.

In May 1970, a protest in the campus of Kent State University in Ohio became a risk after Kent State University's National Guard started shooting at nonconformists, killing four students. The incident prompted vocalist and lyricist Neil Young to compose his shocking dissent song "Ohio." The tune, played by Crosby, Stills, Nash and Young and nassassss the Nixon group. Neil composed the lyrics "Tin fighters and Nixon's on the way! We're finally all by ourselves! This late in spring, I hear the beat of the drum. /Four dead in Ohio!"

Despite these fears they continued to escalate the conflict over the next few years. In the year 1972 Nixon was able to move on with a different strategy to appeal for a war of words on North Vietnam's supporters. Most outstandingly, Richard Nixon

Then, they figured out how to engage in unquestionably high-level discussions to China in what could be the Nixon's unique Cold War "detente." The Nixon visit to China cannot be discounted. The way in which the head of the socialist China was able to openly discuss issues with an American president was a rousing event for all the complexities during that Cold War. It was the first time where an American head of state was aware of as the Chinese socialist government as a tyrannical one, and even sat down for a conversation.

Nixon always the master planner He was fully aware that a wedge been created between the Soviets in the past and Chinese and he was willing to profit from it to the fullest extent the value it could bring. Nixon was aware that a wedge had been created between the two. Nixon knew his position that it was actually the Soviets that were in support of those who supported the North Vietnamese now, not the Chinese government. Nixon was hoping to court China in order to gain more influence, while also arranging an end for Vietnam. Vietnam War.

and his side or his part, socialist Chinese and his part, socialist Chinese Mao Zedong invited the chance to get his own concessions to negotiate to fight the Soviets. Zedong was not committed to negotiating an alternative route for socialist China that was not the one negotiated by Soviet Russia and also urged the possibility of exchange between China and in the United States. Nixon's visit to China marked the beginning of the source of current China-US relations, and established the framework upon which that relationship was created. Although it wasn't able to accomplish much of what it was supposed to accomplish in closing the war in Vietnam the dialogue that Nixon established was a major achievement on its own.

In the meantime it was clear that the North Vietnamese were on the march. In the latter part of March in 1972, they launched their embarrassing Easter Offensive, otherwise called the Nguyen Hue Offensive, which made steps to wipe away the South Vietnamese powers. Nixon was unable to endure this humiliating loss and he resorted to Operation Linebacker, which used massive besieging efforts to defeat North Vietnam. The American force effectively drove North Vietnam back. North Vietnamese back (actually like the linebacker in a football match) to their own side to the DMZ.

In the end, Vietnam War was a real impasse, however this display of determination and power in the face of Nixon finally convinced the Soviets to think about negotiating an agreement for harmony in Vietnam. This turned out to be another political race year in 1972 and Nixon was trying to work out a deal before voters cast their ballot form on the seventh of November. However, in reality, South Vietnam President

Guyen Van Thieu was the one who ended up ruining these plans by pulling out in the last second. In the end, Nixon did not have much to worry about when it was related to his

the re-appointment as he was elected with a greater chance of error than at first. Nixon absolutely hammered senator George McGovern in the well popular vote, and was able to win almost every state of the Union (Nixon took 49 of the 50 states). When you consider the manner in which Nixon was forced to leave his post in humiliation, it's remarkable to consider the amount of people who were able to cast a vote in order to restore his office. However, when Nixon received a new term, the debates between North as well as South Vietnam kept on going in a nonstop fashion. Wanting to break northwards, Nixon occupied with an massive bombardment run on the 14th, better called"Christmas Bombings "Christmas Bombings" (its most common title would be Operation Linebacker II). In the course of time, arrangements became the main focus of the following January. On the 27th of January 1973, a contract was reached between the two sides. However, back in the United States the situation was likely to be a laughing matter for Nixon as the Watergate scandal became public. It was discovered that Nixon was the one who had was able to win the presidential election was sending agents to monitor the Democrats. They had, however, actually gotten in to Washington, DC. Democratic headquarters at Washington, DC. The investigation was conducted, and ultimately led into Nixon himself. Nixon was caught during the saga and was likely going to be accused of being a fraud and ultimately removed from the office. Recognizing that Nixon was in a bad spot the people who worked with him convinced Nixon to resign.

With Nixon as president The North Vietnamese were encouraged to put any previous arrangements by the United States government to be tossed aside. They went straight into Saigon and ended the war not in harmony, but with an out-and-out socialist overthrow. The end of the war was South Vietnam, as Vietnam was joined under a single socialist faith system. The hard-fought conflict of America's Cold War with the Soviet Union was lost. Cold War hero Richard Milhous Nixon was, at the same time, was forced to fade into obscurity.

One year after his decision to renounce his vows, Nixon almost threw up the towel in the summer of 1974 after he was taken to the hospital for an embolism pneumonic. The incident certainly sparked the previously mentioned musician and vocalist and Nixon criminal Neil Young to review a portion of the catch this second. Youthful was fascinating in regards to the life of Nixon. While he criticized Nixon in the dissenting tune "Ohio," Young composed an elegant interpretation of Nixon that was dubbed "Campaigner," which had an edgier tone.

In a reflection on Nixon's fragility Neil Young hauntingly sang, "Emergency clinics are a thing of the past."

caused him to cry. But there's always an expressway in his eyes/Though his oceanside just got overly busy during his walk/Roads are slack as solid veins/Roads become wild present ponies tangle the reins/Where it's true that Richard Nixon has got soul/Even Richard Nixon has soul."

Nixon was, in all likelihood, the most hated person in the world at the moment, in his sad, serious singing voice. Neil was required to intervene and tell us that Nixon was not a monster. He was a human. He fought and performed as any other human being however, whatever he might have done in the past even the hardline adversaries of the socialist Cold War hero Richard Nixon was a person with an ounce of soul.

Chapter 6: A East African Cold War

"I'm an experienced man. I took the actions I did because my country must be freed from tribalism and feudalism. If I failed I did so because I was a double-crosser. The claimed annihilation was simply an issue with regard to the change and the system from which all have gained." Mengistu Haile Mariam

The African area is frequently omitted when discussing the effects from the Cold War, however the Cold War had its effect in this case, and it was no different. The sting from the Cold War was felt the most strongly within East Africa. Somalia is now completely inseparable from war as well as fragile, became a socialist state in the year 1969 when an ex-general from Somalia Somali general known as Mohamed Siad Barre seized power.

immediately, Siad Barre was the love of immediately. Siad Barre was the adoration of Soviet Union and was showered with unqualified guidance. However in the event that one of Somalia's most feared enemies within the Horn of Africa, Ethiopia was also a socialist country the strain was evident all over. Ethiopia is an ancient nationand the only African nation that has never been defeated by a foreign power. The Italians tried to gain control over Ethiopia in two separate instances and failed both times.

Ethiopia has a long and rich history that boasts an extensive lineage Ethiopian rulers who are described being "heads." They Ethiopian rulers are believed to have a lineage that goes all the way to Queen Sheba who is believed to visit the King of Israel Solomon sometime around 959 BCE. According to legend the two proved to be extremely close. In fact, they were close enough to birth a child the Ethiopians were referring to as Menelik (not not to be confused as Menelik II who, in large part, removed his fellow Italians away from Ethiopia during 1898). Menelik was to become the leader of the Ethiopian space and, through him a vast line of lords would govern Ethiopia in the next couple of centuries. The whole thing would come to an end when the final Ethiopian ruler, Haile Selassie, was taken into a social-democratic crisis in 1974. Selassie was the ruler over Ethiopia in the 1930s and was in charge of his country due to the fundamentalist hatred to Italian dictator Benito Mussolini during World

War II He was brought in the Marxist-Leninist group called the Derg.

at the start from the beginning, the head was placed under house arrest, however from the beginning, Derg showed up his defense in 1975 through the execution of the ruler. Selassie was eventually replaced with a lower-ranking official as well as a Derg was replaced by the name from Mengistu Haile Mariam. Prior to the takeover by the socialists, Ethiopia was a solid all-weather partner to the

United States. America was a part of this African secure government as a bulwark against socialistism, and in particular the threat that socialist Somalia.

When Ethiopia transformed into social democratic country, America remove its relations with its former partner and ally in the region. In the meantime, the Soviet Union, obviously, was incredibly happy to accept Ethiopia believing that it would become an important chess piece to their interests in East Africa. Because Somalia and Ethiopia were both socialist countries Somalia as well as Ethiopia were socialist states, the Soviets believed that the two countries would have a strong relationship in their relations with each other. However, Somalia's Siad Barre clearly didn't view the situation as something that could be considered as such. He wanted to expand his own area and was astonished by his Soviet partner when he requested his troops to take on Ethiopia's Ogaden region in 1977. Ogaden is a region that is in dispute which lies to the west of Somalia's boundaries and has a large population that is ethnic Somalis. In the wake of these events it appears that the Soviets were currently an socialist country fighting another socialist nation within East Africa. This was not the kind of scenario the Soviets were expecting. Which of the two would they choose to support? The Soviets were furious over the Somali invasion and also regarded Ethiopia as the most prominent prize, and so they decided to cut down on the support for Somalia and bolster support for Ethiopia instead.

The move was extremely infuriated Somali the pioneer Siad Barre. So much so that in November 1977 Barre sent all Soviet staff members to Somalia to Somalia for pressing. It was perhaps a good thing for Ethiopia because the country needed the assistance of the Soviet Union. The chaos that drove the socialists out of power many of Ethiopia in a shattered state. It was evident that the Ethiopian army was ready for fighting Somalia. In any event after the Soviets dropped billions of dollars of military equipment and sent a large amount of Cuban warriors, demonstrating the civility of Fidel Castro and the Ethiopians were ready to fight. The Ethiopians together with their allies annihilated the Somali army and forced them out of Ethiopia. Somalia needed to see that Ethiopia was in the right direction to Ogaden and gave up any plans to challenge Ethiopia's dominant position in the region. This placed Somalia and the United States in an exceptionally bizarre situation. In during the Cold War, at whatever moment the Soviets stood up for of the sides in a conflict in the war, they United States, nearly of course, would end in the end supporting one side over the other. But, as it happens, Somalia was a socialist country. How can be the United States help socialists? Whatever the tests of supporting socialists in the event that it can help in thwarting Soviets Soviets in the region that it is, this is what the United States chose it

It is worth their time and effort to assist Somalia.

Somalia was of equal importance to Americans due to its location in close proximity to in the Middle East and, specifically in specifically, the Persian Gulf. So they and the United States worked out an agreement in which they provided a essential information to Somalis in exchange for Somalis in exchange for admission to Somalia's air bases and ports located in Mogadishu, Chisimayu (Kismayo) and Berbera. In Ethiopia the socialist government of Mengistu was preparing to accept his aid with assistance from his ally, the Soviet Union, getting billions of dollars of aid throughout the conflict.

In spite of this assistance, Ethiopia was struggling getting up and running. The country was hit by terrible starvation in the 1980s. It was this starvation that triggered the enthralling Live Aid show, which featured a number of superstars singing "We are the World" and made an impressive effort to raise money to support the cause. While it's not entirely that this money actually helped the hungry youngsters and the money went to Mengistu's pocket however the general public attention was focused on the country's struggles through Cold War. Cold War.

It's not entirely surprising that Mengistu was the one who guaranteed an abundance of food for the Ethiopian poor, often did not provide basic nutrition to his relatives. Mengistu began to revert to the famous slogan "Land To the Tiller." This meant that the land of the refined people of Ethiopia would be equally divided and distributed for Ethiopian farmers. But this distribution system was a major problem, in the sense that it affected the entire landscape of horticulture, causing a massive and widespread hunger.

In order to combat the famine which was afflicting his nation, Mengistu started to move Ethiopians from the "dry northern regions" located in mountains to farms in the south of the country during the 1980s. Ethiopians living in the northern regions were particularly hard hit by the famine. This will clearly help the homesteads as well as provide relief for those struggling the most.

Every Ethiopian transported south was promised an individual plot of land, as well as "dairy cattle, seeds compost, clinical assistance for not under one-year." This blunder would have forced the removal of 2 million Ethiopians. This was a huge blow to the Western globe, that at present been an observer to Mengistu's socialist regime, reallocating Western guidelines for hunger to his military was a huge skepticism, to put it mildly.

A deeper reason for Mengistu's part will later be discovered. People in the end realized that the majority of Ethiopians who Mengistu had shifted from the "bone-dry northern regions" came from areas which had been actively opposition to his power. So, it appears that the entire majority of the population was, in a way, intended to stifle the popular opposition to his government.

But, in 2001, no help from the Soviet Union nor innumerable American VIPs who sang "We are The World" could halt the demise of Mengistu Haile Mariam's disastrous socialist system. Another popular unrest was raging in the northern part of Ethiopia in the region of Tigray. It was one of the regions that Mengistu was trying to control. Mengistu was eventually dismissed by a well-known Tigray leader, Meles Zenawi, who was backed by TPLF (Tigray People's Liberation Front). Whatever the extent Mengistu as well as his Marxists tried to force socialism on people who are normally Ethiopian the way they thought, their philosophies were always in conflict with the majority of the population. Certain people believed that the land reform was vital to inspire the workers, however certain aspects of socialism do not work well within Ethiopian society.

In the context of a particular thing, Ethiopia is a profoundly strict country. Ethiopia is a part of Judaism within the Old Testament, and it was among the first countries that became Christian in it was in the New Testament. The underlying principles that are the basis of Ethiopian Orthodox Tewahedo Church, that date back to 300 CE was not likely to be wiped out easily by the communists who were heathen.

Meles Zenawi would enjoy the full support by his fellow members of the Ethiopian Orthodox Church to achieve his goal of driving the socialists from the country. As Meles Zenawi and his political dissidents moved towards the Ethiopian capital city of Addis Ababa and were granted permission to go in "basically without opposition," exhibiting the super level of resentment the country felt towards Mengistu. Mengistu was able to escape to Zimbabwe in the month of May 1991. The Soviet guidebooks and correspondence were immediately cut off.

While Mengistu's system was in the process of self-destructing Americans began to withdraw from Somalia in the wake of the collapse of the regime of Siad Barre was falling apart. Somalia's post-Cold-War future will be a lot less fortunate than the Ethiopians. While Ethiopia was able to transition from a socialist state into an official republic, Somalia went from socialism to total bedlam and rebellion--a situation of a fervent unrest that Somalis are currently trying to escape from. It's an

A tale about the story of two East African nations impacted by the ever-present Cold War.

Chapter 7: Cold War Secrets And A Place Called Area 51

"In any case, during the length of the Cold War, the exceptional confrontation in the middle between Soviet Union and the United States was generally kept clear of any imminent tension between our civilians and, more likely, the military of our countries."

- Vladimir Putin

When the Cold War escalated, so did the mystery surrounding both sides. This was the most apparent with regard to the development of new military equipment. The United States, as the Cold War lingered with inescapable anxiety about Soviet monitoring, those fears of fear prompted the desire to establish a highly secure office in which US designers could work at the latest ingenuity technology free of interruption and unwanted scrutiny. Therefore, a remote section of Nevada desert, which had been designated as such by the US military only as "Region 51" was deemed to be attractive.

prior to it becoming an expo site for military technology, Area 51 was known as the Nevada Test Site. In the years following World War II, this desert area was used for the testing of nuclear bombs. Since the start in the Cold War, the Air Force and CIA were significantly involved, and began working from a region within Area 51 called Groom Lake. In 1955, in Groom Lake, the CIA launched a new project known as AQUATONE. The project AQUATONE was a project to create a covert agent aircraft that could fly through Soviet airspace, and not be identified from Soviet Union. Soviet Union.

It was a few years before Sputnik and spy satellites hadn't yet been developed. In the past, the only way to gain analysis of your opponent was to steal their airspace, and fly right after it was to the other side. Naturally, if US aviation personnel were found to be engaging in this manner and were caught, they would be at risk getting shot, as well as triggering an even more intense battle between their counterparts in the Soviet Union itself. It is not necessary for any nation's airspace to be misused regardless of the circumstances and it was entirely within its rights to take proactive steps.

However, US authorities just needed to know what Soviets were up to and the best method to monitor their foe was to possess an aircraft that could get into Soviet security measures, snap some photos of what was happening at the surface, and then return without being detected. This is what was taking place in Project Aquatone, and it was the responsibility of the designers of Groom Lake to plan an aircraft that could satisfy the requirements. US intelligence

at present, could have a good idea of the components of Soviet air defenses were made of, and discovered that Soviet radars had a limited capability. It was believed that if they were to build an aircraft that could be taken off sufficiently, it would not be recognized by Soviet radar structures. It was within the purpose of this high-height vehicle that the U-2 operational plane of the government was designed. The engineers at the U were not really set in stone the task of making an aircraft that could reach the height of 70,000 feet to enter Soviet airspace without being noticed. Area 51's designers Area 51 quickly surged out their first version of this type in late spring 1955.

Once the process had begun in the beginning, the US military was given the role of a functionally less important one and made CIA specialists fly the specialization instead of overhauling individual soldiers. In the event that the U-2 fell in the event of a crash, it was regarded as normal to use the CIA pilot dressed in customary attire instead of a trooper wearing military fatigues. The reason for this was to allow the army not deny the contribution. It is important to note that the U-2 did not appear like an art of the battlefield. Indeed, the first many to abandon to the construction sequence were marked by an "NACA" emblem. NACA is the acronym for National Advisory Committee for Aeronautics it was a research organization founded in 1915. The group was later transformed to become the natural NASA. In the event that the U-2 was ever required to be a part of a crisis in some location then the CIA had a tale planned to be prepared. If they were spotted they would make sure it was a fake U-2 was an investigation make that focused on meteorological anomalies in the upper atmosphere. In reality, the main reason of U-2 was that the U-2 was to monitor that of the Soviet Union.

The U-2 was able to effectively conduct spying missions across Soviet airspace over the next several years, providing an extensive understanding of things such as locations of troops within Eastern Europe and rocket destinations in Russia. Perhaps the most important aspect that the U-2 government operative plane found was was a major contradiction between the information Soviet revolutionary Nikita Khrushchev claimed to have in relation to nuclear rockets, and what was actually at ground. With the help of the Eisenhower group and the Eisenhower organization, it was discovered that Khrushchev was lying, since his Soviet reserve was in fact much smaller than Khrushchev declared. It was discovered that the radar structures of the Soviet Union were in reality more sophisticated than US planners expected and were doubt able to differentiate the flyovers. However, in all it was the Soviets at the time were not equipped with a rocket or plane capable of sowing enough to block American art. In 1960, the situation became the case when Soviets created a surface-to-air rocket (SAM) that

will eventually get to the top-flying U-2.

This capability was later revealed to the world May 1st of 1960. A 30-year-old pilot with his name Gary Powers was designated by the Soviet's newly created SAM. Gary was flying through the air and snapping photos of Soviet establishments just like the rest of us. Given his elevation of 75,000 feet, he knew that he was completely out of reach for the Soviets. He was shattered when an explosion caused a shake in the plane. The source of the blast was an SAM that detonated beneath the U-2. While this rocket did not hit the plane in a straight line but its shockwaves caused the U-2 lower to a lower elevation.

When this happened that occurred, that happened, Soviets took Gary's expertise once more and sent another SAM speeding right towards Gary. This one was able to track its target. The impact tore the wings of the U-2 right off and sent the remaining parts of Gary's plane to an arc. Because his craft was at such a high altitude in the surroundings, Gary wore a compressed suit that was a kind of archetype for the suits space travellers were later to wear. Because the tension in the art had been eliminated the suit began to be trimmed to redress and made it hard for Gary to change his control.

At first, he thought about pressing the button that released him so that his chair would go soaring from the specialization, like he had planned. But, Gary had been thumped forward within the cockpit so that he realized that if when he pressed that button the legs would smash against the "shelter rails" of the specialization which would surely cut them off and his own body. As the plane was falling violently towards the earth's cold, Gary settled on the decision to simply unzip the cockpit of the specialization and jump out. Unbelievably , from this height, Gary had the option to gently drop rational sound when his parachute was deployed.

It is a remarkable achievement, and one that could be highly praised if it weren't due to the fact that Gary made a crucial entrance. He wasevidently kneeling in a hostile zone and when his feet came into contact with Soviet soil it was clear there was any resistance at all. Gary was quickly spotted by Soviet forces on the ground and was detained. It took a while to find someone who spoke in English perfectly, however, when they did, the cross-examination began.

They asked numerous questions which included one that was about the mysterious "desert base" located in Nevada which Powers was flying from. They had in order to understand Area 51. In reality it was believed that the Soviets were watching the American secretive operative art which began in this remote part of Nevada and came to the realization that it was the scene of the mysterious aircraft of a government agent's turn of events. Despite this, Gary would not

Do not divulge any details about Area 51 and on second believed that he was left California.

Gary initially was able to keep on top of the practiced narrative that he was in essence conducting meteorological tests and was being snubbed over the course. However, once it became apparent that his Soviet supervisors were not likely to believe him eventually, he admitted that he was actually on an investigation with the CIA. In the beginning the Americans were completely in the dark regarding what could be happening to their pilot who was missing. Seven days after Gary's capture, the mystery was discovered after Soviet leader Nikita Khrushchev revealed publically that they owned an American government-operated aircraft and its pilot on their premises.

It was a huge humiliation for the president Eisenhower and forced Eisenhower to finally admit to the fact that the US was in fact controlling observation of the Soviet Union. Gary Powers was put being under investigation in August of 1960. He was sentenced to ten year imprisonment for his treason. For the good of Gary Powers, he was able to be saved by his American supervisors after the "spy trading" was concluded with the other Cold War camps in 1962. Powers was handed back to the Americans as a reward for the Soviet secret operative Rudolf Abel.

The disappointment caused by the U-2 was devastation and causing the residents of Area 51 to return to the planning stage seeking out an aircraft that would not be identified in those of the Soviet Union. It wasn't long after the U-2 disaster that the folks in Groom Lake started dealing with the possibility of"the SR-71

"Blackbird." It was a top specialization, and it appeared to be straight from the pages the pages of Buck Rogers. The end result would have a huge capacity, considering that it could fly at 20,000 feet above the U-2 up to the air outside of the world.

The Blackbird isn't really a spacecraft but it does have the potential to be. It's the highest air-breathing motor that is in the presence. The Blackbird is also fast and has a top speed of 2200 miles per hour. The Blackbird's design wouldn't face the exact issue Gary Powers experienced since, in the event that a rocket was directed towards it target, it could make a quick move and then out-maneuver it! Perhaps, however, more than all the smooth design of the art significantly reduced it's radar's radar-cross-segment (the percentage of how visible an aircraft is to radar).

To clarify to be clear, the Blackbird isn't a secret plane however, it's certainly an indicator. The Blackbird was to be involved in a handful of surveillance missions throughout the Vietnam War, continually remaining one step ahead of the air defenses of the enemy. It's estimated as such that North Vietnamese dispatched some 800

Surface-to-air missiles were launched at Blackbirds during the war but proved to be ineffective, since this innovative specialization could bypass them every time.

The most serious risk the pilot faced while piloting the Blackbird was the specialized failures of their own equipment. This kind of problem was encountered in 1987 when an SR-71 that was being transported off to investigate Soviet installations on the Baltic coast, saw one of its motors suddenly explode. This caused the plane to lose its height as well as the captain was forced to attempt a crisis landing. The closest agreeable location was Sweden. The plane flew into Swedish airspace, and was spotted by the Swedish military based on aviation. After they recognized the aircraft and recognizing it, the Swedes followed the aircraft to Denmark. This gesture would prove fundamental of the Blackbird's primary objective, as it would be discovered that the plane was observed in the air by Russian warplanes. A certain time the Russian MiG-25 was firmly been enthralled by the technology and was in a position to take it down. When the Swedes came to a compromise and mediated, the Russians pulled back, not prepared to risk hitting the

Swedish plane, which allowed the Blackbird to effectively be escorted back to safe. In the latter half of the 1980s in the 1980s, the Pentagon was contemplating the demise of the Blackbird however, there was a replacement in process. The folks at Area 51 were working to complete what they described as"the "miserable gemstone." "The "sad jewelry" was about the new covertness of airplanes' "precious stone molded cross segment," which could avoid radar structures that are based on ground. Engineers understood that the shape of this jewel could be crucial in directing adversary radar, however, they discovered that it was extremely difficult to create a precious stone-shaped art that was ready to fly.

The initial model of what might become a secret military aircraft was called The Have Blue, and it was taken off the sequential structure system during the latter half into the late 1970s. It is possible that the experts thought that it was a disaster, but they held off the assault on the design until they were given the choice of creating an advanced aircraft that had a valuable stone-shaped cross-area, clear wings and internal vertical stabilizers inclined. The final product looked amazing. The general population also agreed. The sightings that have been characterized as such often UFO (unidentified flying object) reports.

The year 1988 was the first time it was revealed to the world the brand new F-117 Nighthawk, a covertness military aircraft, wasn't an extra planet but rather an extremely

Modern cutting-edge aircraft. Declassified today, the aircraft will witness its first major piece of activity in 1991 , during the Gulf War. The aircraft that was classified could have the capability of infiltrating Iraqi airspace with no risk of being punished, causing Saddam Hussein to have his air defenses shoot ferociously in the air, hoping to strike the target at a different time. However the secrecy of the aircraft proved inaccessible during this mission.

With the help of the secret make with the help of the covertness make, it was the United States controlled the air over Iraq and promptly shut the power of Saddam Hussein down. The Soviets were unable to resist the chance to be aware, and began to feel the pressure much more. They

Soviet Union had effectively been fighting to be aware of American military advancements, and had used around a quarter percent of its (GDP) to accomplish the case, but they were essentially outclassed. They did not have an aircraft capable of battling the spies in disguise. It was a surprise that American aircraft were focused on Iraq as they ought to have been deploying against the Soviets because this amazing display of American knowledge and capability has made many people in Russia conscious of the fact that Cold War was everything except lost.

In the past in the past, Russians were scared by the claims of Ronald Reagan's possessing SDI (Strategic Defensive Initiative) space-based weapons that could be used to thwart nuclear weapons. This would prove to be a lot more so a lie as compared to reality however, with the secrecy of competitors, the world was given the undisputed proof of a major advancement in the military side of events. It was also one that the incredibly weak Soviet Union would have no chance of being aware of. Despite the fact that it was not the sole factor, the revelation about the Cold War secret assisted with speeding the end in the Cold War. It was believed that the Soviet

Union would eventually implode prior to the end of 1991.

Chapter 8: Soviets, Afghanistan, And A Bit Of Salt

"During the Cold War, America embraced genuine cuts to military only once: following the election to the office of Richard Nixon, during the Vietnam War. The result: Vietnam was a disaster for Afghanistan and American drastically."

- Ben Shapiro

at the time at the beginning of Cold War, both the United States and the Soviet Union began to build their nuclear weapons at an alarming pace. It was the United States-- the largest country to promote nuclear weapons had the upper hand, but that was not the case when the Soviet Union got up to the speed of light. The Soviets developed its first nukes in the year 1949, and following that, they tested their first nuclear bomb in the year 1955.

there's sometimes a bit of confusion over the distinction between things such a nuclear bomb and a nuclear weapon, therefore let me make it clear. Both are nuclear bombs. However, the nuclear bomb is much more impressive than the nuclear bomb. Nuclear bombs were among the first atomic bombs created which is why it's logical that they're not quite as spectacular as hydrogen bombs. Yet, even nuclear bombs can be capable of massive destruction; take an examination of the nuclear bombs that were dropped on Japan that were amazing to destroy entire cities and claim a numerous lives as a result of the repercussions.

In its most basic definition An Atomic weapon is a weapon that "infers its power to destroy" through atomic reaction. Nuclear bombs accomplish this through breaking up the molecule, whereas nuclear bombs rely on more remarkable combination responses from hydrogen. Before the introduction of intercontinental long range rockets during the final part during the 1950s these weapons had to fall from airplanes. With ICBMs, an atomic-tipped rocket could be destroyed at the touch of one button.

As that both Soviet Union and the United States had ICBMs in their arsenals and ICBMs, both countries exhibited the capability to destroy one another in a condition known as a "commonly guaranteed" destruction. If one country emptied its nuclear rockets, another was sure to follow suit with the result that both of them would both be destroyed at the same time. The obliteration that was usually guaranteed was thought as a definitive test because it ensured that neither teams used their weapons. However, the weapon contest turned dangerously wild. Finally, and for both socialists and the Russians, the Russians entered

All over the world affected all over the world. The sides that were wound down began to get agitated over the massive amount of nuclear weapons they used and sought at ways to reduce the amount of atomic weapons they had. This desire for a reduction that led to SALT (Strategic arms limitation talks). The first SALT agreement, SALT I, was signed on May 26 in 1972. The agreement stipulated that the two parties could limit "the amount of crucial long-range rocket launchers" each nation has and also set limits on the range of IBMs.

It was an advance arrangement that was a trust-building arrangement, and there was a belief it would result in a new arrangement to be added. The next SALT agreement, SALT II, came to fruition in the middle of the year of 1979 under supervision of American President Jimmy Carter and Soviet Premier Leonid Brezhnev. The agreement was much more comprehensive than the previous. It stated that both sides needed to reduce their "essential capabilities" from 2,250 per. But, the plans could be in danger if they attacked the Soviet Union attacked Afghanistan a half a year after.

Soviet powers dominated Afghanistan during Christmas Day, on December 24th 1979. The reason? to aid Afghanistan's young socialist group. Afghanistan had encountered a pseudo-transformation in 1978 known as the Saur Revolution. The Saur Revolution brought a small group of neighborhood Afghan socialists into a position of power to the utter disappointment of a significant portion of the part of the nation. When the discontented Afghans tried to eliminate the socialists however, the Soviets blamed them in order to completely attack the country.

The Soviet occupation and intrusions earned an immediate censure from United States, with President Jimmy Carter criticizing the activities and breaking off all ties to the Soviets. It was a formal end to detente which was the period of less tensions between the two major meetings in the Cold War. Carter was furious to the point where he requested that to have the United States blacklist the Olympic Games in the year 1980. Carter further asked that the Senate be able to consider the suspension of SALT II.

Also, the Americans were not the sole ones to scold Russia and the Soviet Union for their intercession in Afghanistan. China also condemned the Russians as well. The Sino-Soviet divide was long was in process and the two nations were experiencing some tense tensions prior to. China is currently disseminating its displeasure, and was actively supporting the Mujahideen fighters in the field as a way of helping in hindering the activities that were being pursued by Russians.

China was not a fan of the Soviet intrusion for a variety of reasons. However, what irked them most was how close the battle was to home.

Afghanistan is located near northwestern China The activities occurring in the region would be recognized to the Chinese. To show its solidarity to violating Russians, China transparently activated its military at its northern frontiers, located which is located in the Xinjiang region.

Yet, despite this benefit it was clear that the Soviets were not impeded enough to be able to leave Afghanistan. They would stay in Afghanistan for a ten-year period of absurd years, during which time they were able to fend off endless waves of Afghan protests backed by an Islamic organization called the Mujahideen. In many ways it was a Cold War flashpoint gave the United States, which had suffered a great deal of blood and money due to Soviet-backed Vietnamese conflict, a chance to take a smack at its Cold War adversary.

It's a bit impulsive to discuss the current scenario in this way, but this is the reality of the Cold War, all things taken into consideration, was a lot of a blow-for-blow kind of trade. Additionally, US authorities began to openly talk about the ways in which Afghanistan could have been Soviet's Vietnam. An unanswered request from the president Jimmy Carter read, "Our ultimate goal is to eliminate the presence of Soviet soldiers from Afghanistan. No matter if this isn't possible, we must try to ensure that Soviet participation as massive as we can." The CIA began to swiftly help and strengthen Afghan groups of agitators, providing them with weapons, training as well as gaining knowledge. In all likelihood the greatest advancement came at the moment when the US gave the Afghans the launcher that was tucked in on the shoulder called"a "Stinger." Stingers were a type of rocket that could smash Russian art from the sky. Before this breakthrough, Russians took over Afghanistan's skies. The Russians were aware that the new weapons came made by their homeland in the United States, yet they were not going to push more on the issue. In all likelihood it was a matter of taking the abuse and Afghans continuously slammed Russian helicopters and aircrafts from the sky. The Russians got enough and retreated from Afghanistan at the end of 1989 however, they left a huge vacuum that remained afterward. After the Russians quit the country, the agitators- many of whom were Americans-trained warriors -- began to fight for supremacy. It was in the agitation that groups such as AlQaeda became popular.

Al-Qaeda was part of earlier mentioned Mujahideen that was a jihadist advancement against the Soviets that the future engineers of the psychologically oppressed Osama container Laden was a member of. Container Laden was later to lead Al-Qaeda. Because AlQaeda is based on the Mujahideen and the Mujahideen, it was in

In a variety of ways, it is possible to infer that there was a possibility that the CIA has a role in creating Al-Qaeda in a variety of ways, since they are the one who assisted in gaining momentum towards the Russians. This suggests that the US did not intend to prepare what could eventually become an armed militant group. The two of them Jimmy Carter and Ronald Reagan required the Soviets to suffer when they attacked Afghanistan but the consequences continued for years.

Chapter 9: Ronald Reagan And The Evil Empire

"Conquering the Cold War required boldness from people from Central as well as Eastern Europe and what was"the German Democratic Republic, yet it also demanded the determination of the Western partners over many years, when many were tragically not had any hope of coordination between both Germanys as well as Europe."

Angela Merkel

Onald Reagan was an opponent of the hardline approach to the fight against socialism. When Reagan first ran as president during the 1980 election race, he declared that the need to end"the "Vietnam syndrome." It was the belief that the tragic and unending Vietnam War had made a kind of pessimistic attitude among Americans; Reagan accepted these feelings of cynicism that should have been eradicated. The cynicism he felt was a constant trigger for his use of a contentious and savage language towards and against the Soviet Union. This was a position that a portion of his faultfinders felt was pointlessly--and maybe hazardously--forceful. In the same way, during his opening question-and-answer session on January 29 1981 Reagan was seen to appear ready to declare his desire for peace , if the opportunity presented itself. He expressed his openness to "an

significant reduction in the number of nuclear weapons."

Reagan also clarified his belief that the Soviets will continue to take over the world. Reagan declared that "their goal should be the growth of global turmoil and a single-world Socialist (or Communist government." If anyone were to study the works that were taught by Marx or Lenin and Lenin, you will be sure to find their thoughts brimming with this kind of view. An idealistic view of a socialist overall government is never a far distance from any socialist's mind.

By these phrases, Ronald Reagan set a limit and made his point clear. Perhaps the most interesting thing that was gleaned from the first interview Reagan gave to the public was not his opinions but his perception of how the Soviets considered the world. Reagan was able to assure to his Soviet Union would persevere relentlessly in its quest to control the world. Reagan stated, "Presently, as long they are doing that, and they have openly and transparently declared that the most ethical aspect they consider to be the one that can help motivate them and that they assert that they have the authority to commit any wrongdoing and lie, or be a fraud, and to achieve the same, and this is not corrupt, but moral and we are working with them to come up with a different set of standards, I believe that when you collaborate together with them even when you reach an agreement, you will must keep this in your mind."

From the beginning of his administration the president Ronald Reagan clarified that his strategy for dealing with his approach to Cold War would not be the same thing. He believed that the lengthy period of peace during the 1970s hadn't led to any significant re-evaluation of the efforts which was done by the United States put in. Because he was the one the one in charge, he wasn't really was he able to change the direction that the country was in. It wasn't that Reagan didn't value peace or past agreements with the Soviets such as SALT, he generally believed that the Russians did not respect the conditions of these agreements so often that they didn't justify the trouble of maintaining for any length of time.

In order to ease an end to the Cold War through an arms control detente Reagan more sought to increase the stakes. Then, he began to work out an arrangement to take on the Soviets suddenly. Instead of limiting arms and a broader expansion of US military expenditures and try to force to the

Soviets to keep pace. Thus, Reagan was the president that Jimmy Carter dreaded to step and he widened the US weapons stock with items such as neutron bombs, and also dispensed creation to buy more B-1 bombers.

Reagan despite his being selected by a large portion of the American public, triggered an abundance of anxiety and anger among the people who voted against his. They believed that Reagan's hardline stance might trigger nuclear conflict between and Soviet Union. In the wake of the political polarization and hatred towards Reagan many began to worry about his personal security. The fears of those who feared for his security were subsequently realized.

horrifically in an incredibly horrific way on March 30 in 1981, Reagan was killed by the future professional killer just on the outside of the Hilton Hotel in Washington, DC. He was just speaking in The Hilton and was taken by a limousine to transport him to his next location when a violent shooter whose name was John Hinckley Jr. trapped Reagan as well as his escort, and fired. In this incident, Reagan, just as his press secretary James Brady, were struck. Brady was the most horribly hit on the head. Reagan was hit by a slug which bounced off the limousine. The slug hit him in the left arm and the slug piercing into his lung. Special assistance agent Timothy McCarthy and cop Thomas Delahanty also suffered injuries the same day.

When the gunfire was fired, Reagan was driven into the car and raced to the hospital for an urgent check-up. If it weren't for this quick and conclusive act the patient could have died the next day. Despite the fact that Reagan was not struck with an immediate blow however the way his lung was shattered caused extreme internal dying. it was reported that he died.

They said he was "near close to death" at the time he was taken in to George Washington University Hospital. Reagan was stabilized, and he had a stunning recovery.

When he returned to The White House, there was an amazing outpouring of compassion towards Reagan and his critics began to become used to the fact that he was. Being content that he was granted a second chance, Reagan accepted that he was in the position of being able to do something extraordinary. In many ways, he believed luck had bestowed upon him the task of ending this Cold War. In addition, during the speedy task, some even considered that there was evidence that the Soviets had been behind the murder attempt.

It was however immediately apparent it was clear that professional murderer John Hinckley Jr. was an incredibly sad person. Hinckley was clearly enticed by the entertainer Jodie Foster, and believed that killing the president would entice her. If this is interpreted as the thoughts of a crazy person This is because Hinckley was insane. He would end up spending in the next 30 years in a psyche-based remorse to be held accountable for his actions. He was finally released in 2016, because the authorities determined that he was in no way considered a threat to the society.

In any case, following the Americans were able to block Soviet mediation during the assault on Reagan the President Reagan began to contemplate specifically reaching out to him directly to discuss the possibility of contacting his Soviet partner. He actually went as an extent as to write an individual note to Leonid Brezhnev.

However, Reagan was convinced by his secretary Alexander Haig, that this might "convey an unacceptable message." The Soviets are, as a matter of fact were demonstrating their full strength with their hostility to Afghanistan and, considering Reagan was required to demonstrate his strength, the situation was not in general to increase the size of the olive branch. In the end, Haig had an authority reminder drafted. Although it did contain some certain developments in relation to the Soviet Union such as ending the grain ban that damaged the Soviet economy, it also solved issues that were causing concern for America including the Soviet infiltration into Afghanistan. In spite of this primary letter however, the Reagan letter was later included. The letter urged Brezhnev to look at "the basic, common problems of people" which each person addressed jointly. The goal was to break over this Cold War ice with individual kindness and empathy for the common people of both sides of the Iron Curtain.

Only the letter based on strategy received a response from the Soviets and they reacted with a round of

The Reagan organization shook off all focus points of the Reagan group had put forth. Disappointed as he was, Reagan was presently genuinely ready to end his tangle and negotiating with Soviets. As such Reagan had the cautious and thoughtful Haig replaced by the more militant George Shultz. Shultz was appointed Reagan's secretary of state at the end of the spring of 1982. from then on, Reagan indeed accepted a much more unpopular position in relation to Russia and the Soviet Union.

Around this time, Reagan made one of his most fanciful revelations as to how he envisioned the end in this Cold War would come to the realization. In a trip to England Reagan proclaimed his belief that the Cold War was "the path of opportunities and the majority rules system which would leave Marxism-Leninism on the history's debris pile since it had left a variety of oppressive regimes that block the possibility and limit the self-expression of people." In the year following the year 1983, his views were clearly thinking of that the Soviet Union an "Malicious Empire."

The extreme rhetoric frightened an en masse portion of the public who believed that Reagan's saber-shaking would trigger an nuclear trading deal between these two giants. The result was a couple of enemies of war fighting to break out both in Europe and the United States and Europe during Reagan's first term. Reagan's daughter Patti participated in the protests.

Although not as bizarre in the same way as his Cold War methodology would have seemed at that time, Reagan knew what he was doing. Reagan outlined his goals by putting them in National Security Decision Directive 75. The stated goals of the order were as follows.

To control and in the long haul reverse Soviet expansionism by battling in a logical and logical manner against the Soviet Union in every area, particularly in the overall balance of military power and topographical areas of for and from the United States. This will remain the primary focus in the U.S. strategy toward the USSR. To accelerate, as much as is possible for us to, the path of advancement within the Soviet Union toward a more pluralistic financial and political structure in which the power of the most favored decision-making class is decreasing steadily. In the end, U.S. perceives that Soviet power has deep roots within the framework that surrounds it and that its interactions with USSR should be evaluated accordingly whether they can help to strengthen this framework and the ability of the USSR to take part in conflict. In order to bring on and include the Soviet Union in arrangements to try to reach agreements that safeguard and strengthen U.S. interests and which conform to the guidelines of strict communication and shared interests. This is crucial.

in the time that there is a time when the Soviet Union is amidst a process of political succession. shortly after this mandate went out Secretary of State Shultz sent out a message concerning relations between the US and Soviet Union in 1983. This document "called for a reversal of the recent Soviet militants by launching an intensified dialogue in dialogue with Moscow." The discussion should focus on "authenticity and common interest." Reagan's "genuine political twang" in actual life that he tried to connect with the Soviets easily and in a pragmatic method to discover what shared beliefs could be achieved.

The first source was the correspondence of a Soviet minister identified as Anatoly Dobrynin. The correspondence was deemed as essential and on the 15th of June in 1983 Shultz his own words stated as many times when he announced the correspondence in front of Congress: "In the beyond two years, the nation... have established an essential

obligation to restore its financial, military and moral force. In addition, having begun to alter our stance on solidarity, we are looking to bring in Soviet innovators for a beneficial exchange, which will allow us to find political solutions to the most difficult questions."

But, by the end of 1983, talks with the Soviets did not go positive. The Russians have been stomping around during discussions of reductions in arms at Geneva, Switzerland. A skeptics' fear of a renewed arms race would be the central role in the public during Reagan's quest to re-appoint him in 1984. The rival, Walter Mondale, would need an atomic ban as well as portraying Reagan as insane during the course of his Cold War procedure with the Soviets. At the end of the day, buoyed by a rising economy and a growing sense of pride that was felt by every American, Reagan was allowed an additional term. This, however, Reagan did win with a total snowball, as he took 49 states out of fifty. He believed that he received an appropriate order by people in the American public to finish what he began.

It was during the Reagan administration that a second Soviet chief, by his name Mikhail Gorbachev would ascend to the top of the list. Mikhail Gorbachev would substantiate himself to be merely the Cold War accomplice that President Ronald Reagan expected to destroy the "Insidious Empire" one and for all.

Chapter 10: The Early Definition Of Events

Before World War II was over and the war was over, each of the U.S. and the U.S.S.R. which were nominally allies in the fight against common enemieshad reasons to doubt and be afraid of each other. In the early years following the end of the war the suspicions and fears intensified into active and intense tensions. Thus, in a literal sense it was that's how the Cold War began even as World War II was ending.

For instance in February 1945 the Allies came together at Yalta located in Russian Crimea to plan for the ending of War in Europe. In Yalta, Stalin informed Churchill and Roosevelt that he wasn't willing to give up the territories in Eastern Europe that the Soviets took in pushing the Germans to retreat towards Stalingrad up to Berlin. Stalin was planning to use the area as a buffer to stop any further Western incursions into Russia. The territory was amounted to more than 150,000 sq miles of land that today is now Romania, Hungary, the Czech Republic, Slovakia, Belarus and Poland. The U.S. not in a position to pressure the Soviets to surrender the land, but it also needed Stalin's aid to conclude this War in the Pacific, that was far from ending. So, Roosevelt made a fateful deal.

Stalin was able to keep Eastern Europe. In exchange, he could transfer his forces to the Asian battlefield within 90 days from the end in the War in Europe in order to aid to help the U.S. defeat Japan. This War in Europe ended on May 8th in 1945. Two months later, in the month of July 1945 the U.S. exploded the first Atomic bomb at Alamogordo, New Mexico. In the end, it didn't need Stalin's support anymore to stop the conflict within the Pacific. The bomb was hurriedly put into operation at Hiroshima on the 6th of August 1945, 89 days following the victory in Europe. The second bomb went off in Nagasaki just three days later, on the 9th. Japanese Emperor Hirohito declared the surrender of Japan on August 15th.

A number of the top U.S. military officials including Dwight Eisenhower, Chester Nimitz, William Leahy, and Curtis LeMay would later state that the bombs hadn't been required to stop the War. Japan was, to all intents and purposes having been defeated, and seeking for peace. However, it was the U.S. wanted to insure that it didn't have to fight in a World War to defeat the fascists but then surrender it to communists. Thus it was important that the U.S. would not allow the Soviet Union to gain territory in East Asia as it had in Eastern Europe. After ending the War by bombing in 1945, it was the U.S. then excluded the Soviets from discussions on settlements in the Pacific area, despite their acceptance in Yalta to include the Soviets.

The month of February, 1946 just six months after the conclusion of War, Winston Churchill declared that the "Iron Curtain" was falling across Europe. He was refers to the Soviet area of influence in Eastern Europe. He declared that It is an act of "will God" God" that nuclear weapons were handed over for the United States and "not a communist state." He stated that the "fraternal group of English people who speak English" should make use of this power nuclear bomb to transform the world beyond the restrictions that are imposed by the United Nations and place it under the control of Anglo-American powerhouses.

According to Stalin it was a declaration of a crypto-racist nature that was similar to Hitler's insane speculations regarding the existence of a "master race." This was his opinion that it was an explicit threat of conflict with Soviet Union. Soviet Union and a betrayal of the agreements reached during the War and reflected the sacrifices that were made to achieve victory in the War and which he was, for his part still honored. While the Soviet the sphere of influence was signed through Roosevelt as well as Churchill in the course of War however, they hadn't anticipated the speed at that it would be established.

In the early days of 1947 Greece began to slide towards collapse with its communist government threatening to deport the country into the Soviet bloc. U.S. President Harry Truman supported the dictatorship with $260 million of aid, however, the government was unpopular and corrupt, as it was losing its civil war battle to communists. Truman was able to respond with what came to be called Truman Doctrine. Truman Doctrine. In the month of March 1947, he declared in his U.S. Senate, "It is an official policy for that United States to support free people who oppose attempts to subjugation by minorities armed with guns or external pressures."

In reality it is true that the Soviets weren't involved with the Greek civil conflict. In fact, Stalin was honoring his agreement of 1944 with Churchill to divide the region. The agreement included British control over Greece as a condition for Soviet control over Romania. But the tone of fear in Truman's speech scared members of the U.S. Congress, which quickly ratified his open-ended plans. It was the Truman Doctrine proved the beginning on the U.S. side of the aggressive policies that were the basis of that Cold War.

The economic wing of the Truman Doctrine was also launched in 1947. In 1947, the Marshall Plan, proposed by U.S. Secretary of State George Marshall, gave economic assistance for the economics that were thriving in Western Europe. They weren't recovering fast enough to provide employment for all their citizens and political turmoil could be a threat. The Marshall Plan has pumped $13 billion into the economies of Europe's capitalists and helped to ward off the lures of communist political parties in the country. Although there was a chance that the Soviet Union had been invited by the French to be a part of in the Marshall Plan, it declined with the belief, along with some argument the Marshall Plan was just a scheme to cause a wedge between it and it Eastern European satellites.

In 1947 In 1947, in 1947, the U.S. settled on what was to be its strategy plan to guide the Cold War. This was the concept called "Containment," devised by George Kennan, Director of the State Department's Policy Planning Staff. Containment stipulated an era in which the U.S. would confront the Soviet Union militarily, politically as well as economically wherever it sought to expand its territory beyond its current territorial boundaries. Korean and Vietnam were one of the most dramatic examples of Containment. However, there would be many lesser-incendiary incidents during the course of the Cold War unfolded.

in 1948 American as well as British authorities declared the unification of their sections of in occupied Germany as well as a plan to create the creation of a modern German currency. The Soviets were not in any way consulted about either of these issues which was a right they claimed from the 1945 accord that was signed by those Allies in Potsdam. They responded by imposing a blockade against Berlin which was situated within the Soviet-controlled region of Germany. Germany. However, the Western Allies countered with the Berlin Airlift. This incident put both East and West together on a hair-trigger axis for 16 months, and created a bitter legacy that shaped relations for years to follow.

Two incidents were witnessed that rocked U.S. to its foundations. First was the detonation from an atomic weapon in the Soviet Union. Just two weeks before authorities from the U.S. Central Intelligence Agency had predicted that they could not be able to achieve this feat for three years. However, it was revealed that the Soviet Union had been aided by spies who had managed to smuggle nuclear secrets from the U.S. The fact that spies were spying revealed a serious vulnerability of the comparatively open U.S. society. Equally harmful was this also meant that U.S. monopoly on nuclear weapons, upon the basis of which it tried to make it difficult for those in the Soviet Union, was broken.

The second thing that happened in 1949 that shaken U.S.'s confidence was the downfall of China. Since the 1930s , the right-wing government in China was involved to a conflict communist revolutionaries. The communists were controlled by Mao Zedong, the government was ruled by the dictatorship of Chiang Kai-shek, the general who. Chiang Kai-shek was the leader of the communists. U.S. had done everything it could to help the nationalists, including sending them money and weapons as well as air support. However, the efforts had not succeeded. Along with Soviet control over Russia and the recent Indian decision in favor of the socialist party which left nearly half the population of the globe and the majority of Asia under the control of communist or socialist-run government. The course of history appeared to be raging against the U.S.

The year was 1950 when the communist regime from North Korea invaded the South intent on bringing the nation under communist control. However, the U.S. replied by sending an army under the direction that of World War II hero, General Douglas MacArthur. When MacArthur was pushed to closer to Chinese border and the Chinese sent more than 2 million troops streaming across the border, pushing U.S. forces back down the peninsula, and nearly losing an entire U.S. the War. In the Korean War lasted until 1953 when an armistice was signed to end the war. However, there hasn't had a peace agreement that was signed. North Korea and South Korea remain officially in an uneasy state even today.

In 1953 in 1953, in 1953, the Soviet Union exploded a hydrogen bomb. It was the same year as the explosion of U.S.'s first H-bomb in just nine months, in comparison to the four years Russia took in blasting its first A-bomb. The Soviet H-bomb was far more advanced than the U.S.'s that used lithium to increase the explosive power. It was a scary sign for the Soviets to be coming with, or even exceeding the West. In 1957 it was the year that the Soviet Union launched the first satellite into space. It flew over with the U.S. four times as it circled Earth. Sputnik provoked a resounding reaction within Western nations and created the inescapable anxiety of the West was in the process of losing Cold War.

This first decade of crucial importance following the conclusion of World War II shattered the American people's hopes of being able to retreat behind two oceans of solitary like they did at the conclusion in World War I. Instead the demands of global leadership (and the possibilities of dominance over the world) demanded engagement from America that it been forced to accept prior to. This new role was not easy initially. It imposed enormous pressures to the American economy and its political system as well as its culture and its society, which all drastically altered by the time it was clear that the Cold War was over.

Chapter 11: Major Events And Battlegrounds

The "hot hot spots" in "hot areas" in the Cold War almost define the second half of the 20th century. These include iconic events such like The Berlin Blockade, the Korean War, Sputnik, the Cuban Missile Crisis, the Vietnam War, and Afghanistan. Each of these events was a distinct battlefield in the larger War which reflected the more complex conflicts that fueled it.

Berlin Blockade

In the Potsdam meeting in 1945 The Allies decided to break up Germany in four "sectors," one controlled by each of the U.S., England, France along with The Soviet Union. Berlin was the capital of Germany was located within the Soviet sector. It was also divided into four parts. In 1948, relations with those of the Soviets with the West had become more strained. In June in 1948, the Allies introduced an entirely new currency for "West" Germany but the Soviets were not been given a chance to speak, refused to accept. Instead, they resisted and blocked Berlin and closed it off to all traffic coming from the Allies sectors. The Blockade threatened to destabilize the democratically elected administration that was in place within West Berlin because it made Berlin completely dependent upon Soviet supplies. Soviet sector for its daily supplies.

In reaction In response, the Allies under the leadership of England and the U.S. and England, set up an airlift to carry supplies to West Berlin. The task was enormous. The city consumed millions of tons of coal, food oil and other items every day. The airlift was initially small, however by the end of October, it was operating hundreds of flights every day. In December airplanes were landing at least minute throughout the day, providing West Berlin with over 4,000 tons of material daily. The airlift was supposed to last just one or two months, but it was actually 16 months, and accounted for more than 230,000 flights. The Soviets eventually surrendered to their blockade.

The war pushed both sides to what they'd be in for the following 40 years. The Soviets attempted to thwart Allied trade integration believing that these moves were designed to break them away from the eastern satellites. The Allies on their own were not averse to being intimidated. Instead, they showed the remarkable technological and economic capabilities to the West to withstand Soviet intimidation. It was the Berlin Blockade proved a dramatic prelude to the outcome and course of the Cold War.

China Changes Communist

In 1919 and on, China had been embroiled in a civil conflict. The initial purpose was to eliminate foreign powers who had been manipulating China for more than 100 years. In 1927, however it turned into an armed conflict between communists led by Mao Zedong and "nationalists" who were led by Chiang Kai-shek. The communists enjoyed a large base within the hundreds of millions of peasants living in the countryside, while nationalists gained their most significant support from the commercial elite and the wealthy property owners in cities. Both sides joined forces in fighting the Japanese invasion to China throughout World War II.

In the immediate aftermath of World War II, the civil war was rekindled with the communists quickly taking the advantage. In the aftermath of World War II, the U.S. provided billions of dollars of assistance and tons of weapons to the nationalists. It also sent more than 100,000 troops to battle the nationalists to take control of Manchuria. Nationalists fell the communists however initially in Manchuria and then in the south in Nanking, the capital of the nationalists of Nanking. In October 1949, communists established as the People's Republic of China in the capital city of Beijing. The leaders of the nationalist party left the mainland for Formosa, an island province in modern day Taiwan. There, they established an alternative government that exists in the present.

"In the end, China's "loss" in China was a major setback towards both China and U.S. First, with

Soviet control of the west and north and Chinese control of East Asia, this put the vast majority of Asia -- and over half the earth's population in the hands of communist-controlled governments. It also seemed to demonstrate to countries in those in the emerging world, that the system of communists was more efficient than capitalism in liberating them from colonial dominance. In addition, it presented grave dangers to the last independent countries of Asia, including Japan, India, the oil-rich countries from the Middle East, and, in particular, the smaller state of Indochina.

Korean War

Korea was split into south and north as part of the resolution in World War II. In the 1950s, the Soviet Union controlled the north and in 1948 established an official communist regime. Then, in June of 1950 the government equipped with tanks, artillery, and tanks supplied by the Soviet Union, and aircrafts and aircraft, invaded South Korea in an attempt to bring this country that was under communist government. It was the U.S. responded by sending its U.S. army under the general Douglas MacArthur. MacArthur prevented the advance by the invaders from northern Korea. However, MacArthur committed a mistake of strategic planning in pushing the invaders north towards north of the Yalu River, the border between North Korea and China.

The Chinese took action by throwing two million troops against U.S. forces, pushing them away from on the Korean peninsula, nearly to the port city in the south, Pusan. But the U.S. pushed back and an impasse was reached that ran until an armistice agreed upon in the summer of 1953. The armistice reestablished the original division line, known as the 38th parallel, which in the present defines the boundary between North as well as South. It was estimated that the U.S. lost approximately 50,000 soldiers during Korea.

Following World War II, the U.S. had quickly demilitarized and reduced its military by three quarters , and its navy in active service by 80percent. Korea was able to take it U.S. by surprise. In the years 1950-53 between 1950 and 1953, the U.S. rapidly rebuilt its army, boosting its army by a half and increasing its military expenditure by a third. In the Korean War is notable, for this reason, because it was the time when it was that the U.S. policy of Containment was put to the first test and saw its first major success. Following Korea however, it was clear that the U.S. never significantly reduced the magnitude of its military involvement until the conclusion of the Cold War.

Korea is notable due to another thing. Because Korea coming so close to the collapse of China the issue was viewed as a matter of politics. Republicans in the U.S. Congress began challenging the competence and even the patriotism of the Democratic-controlled Truman administration. This led to the "communist terror" as well as "communist scare" and "witch hunts" that were associated with Wisconsin senator Joseph McCarthy (see below) in which the national security issue was utilized to gain political advantage. The repercussions of this time remain in the political sphere in this U.S. today.

Cuban Missile Crisis

In 1959 President Batista, who was corrupt in his position from Cuba, Fulgencio Batista, was ousted by a young Nationalist Fidel Castro. While Castro was not an avowed communist, he took over properties that was owned through U.S.

corporations. As a retaliation, U.S. imposed an embargo on Cuban sugar which is the main export of the island. Castro sought out the Soviet Union for help and was immediately welcomed by its leader Nikita Khrushchev. A communist regime located so in close proximity to the coasts of United States was both an embarrassing and a danger for the U.S.

In the month of October, 1962 in the month of October 1962, it was discovered that the U.S. discovered that missile launch sites were being built in Cuba located just 90 miles away from mainland U.S. mainland. Khrushchev had ordered the sites to be constructed in reaction the U.S. missile sites having been set up in Turkey right towards the southern part of the Soviet Union. U.S military forces were placed to "DEFCON 2" alert, which was the most advanced state of readiness that was not required for an actual war. It was the only moment in the entire period of 45 years in the Cold War they were placed at this level of alert. Strategic Air Command B-52 bombers were equipped with nuclear weapons. U.S. Polaris submarines were similarly prepared for nuclear war.

The U.S declared the issuance of a "quarantine," or blockade in Cuba and demanded that the Soviets to dismantle the missiles. The Soviets did not agree. In the end, convinced that the threat of nuclear war, Kennedy agreed to a secret deal in which it was agreed that the U.S. would remove its missiles from Turkey in exchange in exchange for the Soviets detaching their missiles from Cuba. However, there was a catch to the deal: the Soviets must agree to keep the agreement secret to ensure that the U.S. would not lose credibility with it NATO allies. Khrushchev agreed , and war was avoided.

The Cuban Missile Crisis was the closest the two superpowers got to a real nuclear conflict. U.S. Secretary of Defense, Robert McNamara, later stated that he was convinced at the time that he could never live another week. The incident alerted both sides of the issue from nukes "brinkmanship" and resulted in greater effort to stay clear of direct conflicts.

Middle East Conflicts Middle East

Since the beginning of World War I, the Middle East has been prized because of its oil, the vital ingredient of industrialization. A few of Roosevelt's most senior advisors wrote to the president that controlling Middle East oil would mean "substantial control over the entire global economy." The 1945 U.S. State Department memo declared the following "Arab oil resources represent an incredible supply of strategically powerful power and are among the most valuable physical prizes in the history of mankind."

At the close in World War II, the regional importance of the region had grown more drastically, since during the War it was discovered that the U.S. had concluded that its oil reserves were depleted. It was in need of a substantial steady supply of oil for its industrial, commercial and military machinery after the war.

From the beginning, the countries of the Middle East lined up on either side during the Cold War. A number of countries, such as Egypt, Syria, Libya, Sudan, Iraq, and Yemen were attempting to escape the sway imposed by colonial powers of the past. After these attempts were (not surprising) rejected by colonial power itself and they sought the Soviet Union for help. The Soviets were willing to help. This led to one of the most important aspects during the Cold War: the battle for the Middle East.

In February 1945 In February 1945, President Roosevelt had a meeting with Abdul ibn Saud, the head of Saudi Arabia. Roosevelt assured Saud U.S. protection of the Saudi royal family in exchange for steady acces to Saudi Arabia's huge oil reserves (Saudi Arabia has the biggest proved reserves of oil worldwide). Then, until 2003 in 2003, in 2003, the U.S. maintained troops in Saudi Arabia to prop up the ruling family that was not popular. Osama bin Laden had cited an occupation carried out by the U.S. of the holiest spot in Islam which is located within Saudi Arabia, as one of the main reasons behind the 9/11 terrorist attacks on the World Trade Center in New York City.

The Iranian Premier, Mohamed Mosaddegh, nationalized the oil production of the country in 1953 The U.S. CIA staged a coup d'etat to remove Mosaddegh to be replaced by the U.S. friend, Shah Reza Palavi. It was the U.S. assisted a military coup in Iraq in 1963, which was aimed at removing Kareem Qasim. As his replacement, the

U.S. erected the Ba'ath party, which was to be led by the future president, Saddam Hussein, became an unreliable U.S. ally until his unwise invasion of Kuwait in the year 1990. In 1967, when the country was in the middle of an important conflict in Vietnam and Vietnam, in the midst of Vietnam's war, the U.S. threw its support to Israel during the Six Day War against Egypt, Jordan, Syria, and Lebanon. This strategic inclination towards Israel in the role of U.S. "deputy" within the Middle East has continued to the present day.

A religious revolution in Iran removed an U.S.-installed Shah and put in his place the first Islamic fundamentalist government within the Middle East, under the direction by Khomeini. Ayatollah Khomeini. In the event that Iran began the war against Iraq in 1980 and it was the U.S. backed Iraq's Saddam Hussein by providing biological weapons, satellite imagery as well as battlefield assistance. In 1980 the president Carter announced his "Carter Doctrine" in response to the Soviet invasion of Afghanistan (see below). The Carter Doctrine stipulated it was the position of U.S. would view as an imminent danger to security rights in the United States any country trying to control the Persian Gulf.

Vietnam War

Following Korea, Vietnam was surely the "hottest" of all conflicts of the Cold War. Vietnam was previously a French colony before and following World War II. Vietnamese leaders had met with U.S. President Truman in 1946 to ask for assistance in securing their freedom of French dominion. However, Truman was afraid of losing French support for Russian communism within Europe was adamant about assisting his fellow French instead. This decision would inflict a grave sour taste on Vietnamese opinions of their relationship with the U.S. and would make it impossible for the U.S. to ever "win the hearts and minds" of the Vietnamese population.

After the French were exiled from Vietnam in 1954 In 1954, the U.S. took over the battle. They claimed their mission was to combat communism, but the communists from North Vietnam were successful in depicting that the U.S. as just another colonial occupier. From 1954 until 1965, from 1954 to 1965, the U.S. supported anti-communist governments that it established throughout the South. However, in 1965, dissatisfied with the inability of these governments to stop the spread of communism, it changed its strategies and started fighting the war. In 1969 there were the number of 543,000 U.S. soldiers were stationed in Vietnam fighting another battle in Asia.

Despite this huge increase in the amount of spending thousands of tonnes of munitions , and hundreds of billions in expenses however, it was clear that the U.S. did not have an effective strategy to win the war. In addition, protests that were major during the War were raging throughout America. U.S., undermining the government's mandate to fight. In 1969 it was the year that U.S. began withdrawing its troops and left this War to be carried out with an army of the South Vietnamese army. In 1973 in 1973, the U.S. military left the country completely. Three million Southeast Asians were killed during the war. It was estimated that the U.S. lost 58,000 men. The year 1975 was the one when Vietnam was ruled by communists.

The Vietnam War is noteworthy for four reasons. The first is that this was the sole war that the U.S. had ever lost until that point during its long history. In addition, it demonstrated the limitations that the Containment principle that been driving U.S. strategy from the start of Cold War. It showed the limitations of technology and money when confronted with the determination of a nation's people to achieve national independence. In addition, it demonstrated that in a democracy the war cannot last if it is supported by the populace. If that support was squandered through those in the U.S. government, the War was also lost.

Afghanistan

Afghanistan is located situated in central Asia has been a battlefield in the war between Russia as well as the West for many centuries. In the late 1970s the fundamentalist Islamic movement was formed to oppose the pro-Western government. The Soviets had a fear of Islamic states along the southern border since majority of those living who lived in its southern regions were Muslims. They were also radicals who were against their "godless" characteristics of communism and fought actions of sabotage and terror in opposition to those who supported the Soviet Union. This threatened the legitimacy that was the Soviet system and fuelled Soviet anxiety about Islamic states that bordered its borders.

The year 1978 saw a military coup orchestrated by Soviet-trained generals took down the pro-Western regime in Afghanistan. The leaders of the coup sought assistance from Moscow in repressing those who were Islamic militants. Moscow was quick to respond on Christmas Day 1979 by deploying thousands of tanks as well as tens and thousands of troops. The reaction of America United States was dramatic. The president Carter declared the war "the most grave menace to peace that had been experienced since Second World War." The U.S. believed, wrongly that it was the Soviet Union was making a attempt to take control of in the Persian Gulf, source of 50 percent of the world's oil.

Chapter 12: Themes Of Major Themes

While the instances that took place during and during the Cold War defined its milestones and its main themes established its nature. The themes range from the wars within the "Third World" (itself the invention of during the Cold War) and McCarthyism as well as arms races as well as economic conflict and detente. The themes and the events that shaped that Cold War largely defined global cultural trends in the second part of the 20th century.

A World-Wide War

World War I was essentially an European War. World War II included the Pacific theatre and some parts of North Africa but was still restricted on Europe in addition to the Pacific route to Asia. It was the Cold War on the other is a World-Wide War.

The Cold War included armed hostilities across every continent of the globe, with the exception of Antarctica as well as Australia. The main lines of conflict were outlined by Europe as well as many of the crucial combats were fought there.

However, fierce battles were engaged within East as well as Southeast Asia, in Korea, China, Vietnam, Laos, Cambodia, Indonesia and Malaysia. Southwestern Asia was the site of numerous conflicts, with a number that remain unresolved. This includes the ones located in Turkey, Lebanon, Israel, Iran, and Iraq.

Africa was the site of many conflicts that fought between East as well as West usually in the hands of Americans as well as the Soviets employing local troops as a proxy for their own troops. Nigeria, Angola, Egypt, Congo and Ethiopia are the most prominent examples of this type of fighting. The wars that took place within South as well as Central America were frequently fought in the context of the greater Soviet against American conflict. While not as many were killed during the Cold War as did in World War II, the duration, the size of the conflict, the stakes and the risk created a more dangerous war for the whole world.

The Last European Civil War

In the year 1945 Europe suffered the ravages of three civil wars in the continent within just 150 years including three civil wars in just 150 years: the Napoleonic Wars; World War I as well as World War II. But, out of the same ashes grew the seeds for a new war, to be fought by two descendants that remain of European civilization: one from the Westand other from East.

The United States was genetically a true descendant of Europe. It was created as an full manifestation of European Enlightenment and grew to maturation in the sciences of capitalism, democracy and democracy which throughout the world only Europe had created. It was a Soviet Union was less fully European it was an amalgamation that incorporated European, Slavic and Asian influences. But the communism that shaped its ideology was completely European reflecting Karl Marx's view of the development of industrial capitalism.

Europe was not just the seedbed, but the site of several of the War's most important combats. The Soviets were the sole rulers parts of Eastern Europe and dominated conflicts in Poland, Hungary, Czechoslovakia, East Germany and Romania. Communist groups fought fierce underground fights within France, Italy, and

Greece. As the War expanded beyond the boundaries of Europe and into China, Africa, the Middle East, and South America the war was constantly supported by one or the other of these gladiators whose origins were in Europe.

Containment

The policy that guided U.S. policy during the Cold War was known as "Containment." Containment was developed through George F. Kennan, who was a former official at the U.S Embassy in Moscow. The first time it was formulated was through his "Long Telegram" to the State Department from Moscow in February 1946. The idea was that the Soviet Union possessed an "inherently sensitive view of world affairs." In the end according to Kennan the Soviet Union was not able to work or compromise with Western nations. The Russians According to Kennan were "impervious to logic, but extremely vulnerable to logic and force."

The implications for policy of Containment were directly derived from the last sentence The U.S. must confront Soviet aggression wherever it happened. Over the next 20 years U.S. foreign and military policy will follow this guidance. Within the Berlin Blockade and across Italy, Greece, Turkey, Iran, Korea, Vietnam, Cuba, in the Middle East, and in many other countries around the globe in which and in dozens of other places around the world, the U.S. would seek to block Soviet developments and undermine governments that are perceived as favoring Moscow.

In 1959 in the year 1959, in 1959, the U.S. was operating over 1400 military facilities around the Soviet Union, from Canada, Greenland and West Germany in the west all the way to Turkey, Pakistan, South Korea, Taiwan and Japan. Around two hundred and seventy of these bases had bombers, missiles or submarines that could deliver nuclear weapons. The huge base network that surrounded this region of the Soviet Union was the direct definition of Containment in military terms.

McCarthyism

The initial Soviet gains after the end of the War resulted in an atmosphere of near-hysteria within Washington. This was created by right-wing demagogues who viewed Roosevelt's New Deal, child labor laws as well as women's suffrage as communist-inspired "red plans." They asserted that communist spies from Soviet-controlled Russia had penetrated the top and most powerful levels of U.S. government, including the State and Defense Departments, and were working towards the destruction of the U.S. itself. The most well-known of these spies were Republican U.S. Senator Joseph McCarthy.

McCarthy used his position as Chairman of the Senate Committee on Governmental Operations to conduct a series of what became known as "witch hunts," sham hearings in which hundreds of people were smeared as being communists or communist-sympathizers. These hearings were used as a tool to discredit political opponents with the use of rumors, innuendos non-substantiated charges and guilt through the act of association. It was the FBI under the direction of its staunchly anticommunist chief, J. Edgar Hoover helped McCarthy's cause by forged records, illegal searches and whispering campaigns against all types of liberals and centrists.

McCarthy's actions and allegations were unquestioned for years, until McCarthy was criticized by powerful opposition. In the year Harry Truman left office, Truman declared:

"It is now evident that the present administrationhas fully embraced, for political advantage,McCarthyism...It is the corruption of truth,the abandonment of the due process of law. It's the application to spread the big Lie...It is the growing the power of the demagogue who lives in the shadows of untruth, the spread of fear and loss of faith at every degree that society."

Although thousands of people lost their jobs and their careers destroyed however, none of McCarthy's sensational accusations were ever proved. In 1954, McCarthy was sanctioned to the Senate for a violation of ethics and showing disrespect toward the Senate. A number of laws written under the influence of the hysterical mania of McCarthyism have been later found in violation of the Constitution. Arthur Miller wrote the play The Crucible, to characterize the extent to which a society that is that is under pressure can be controlled by those with "theological" control and seeking to wield illegitimate power.

However, the stories of the ease with which people had been destroyed shocked several prominent politicians, like John Kennedy Lyndon Johnson, and Richard Nixon, all of who vowed to never be viewed as "soft against the communist ideology." This determination caused both of them to extend their involvement in the Vietnam War long after it was discovered to have been lost.

Anti-Colonial/Anti-Imperial Complications

The Cold War was primarily about the war with Soviet as well as American systems. However, the major combat was not within the "First World" of the U.S. and its allies as well as inside the "Second World" of the Soviets and its allies however, within the "Third World"--in Asia, the Middle East, Africa and South America. It was at this time that the countries of these regions were emancipating themselves from European colonial influence. These were the prize that both sides in the Cold War fought.

In the Third World, "Wars of National Liberation" were funded through the Soviet as well as later Chinese governments. Following World War II,

British colonies in Burma, India, Pakistan as well as Nepal all sought to gain independence. They all would either fight or choose communist- or socialist-leaning regimes. In 1949 the Dutch attempt to regain the control over Indonesia against a nationalist-led communist insurgency resulted in one the most bloody, long-lasting combats in the Cold War. Before Vietnam was considered a U.S. war to contain communism, it was actually a war fought by the Vietnamese to take over from the French who had occupied the country for more than 100 years. This was also true for Vietnam's neighboring countries, Laos and Cambodia.

In Africa these wars developed into the norm. Between 1960 between 1960 and 1964 England suffered losses in Nigeria, Kenya, Botswana, and Rhodesia and all of them were ruled by communist factions fighting. The battles in Angola and Ethiopia the fighting continued for years and both the U.S. and Soviet Union as proxies and supplying them with aid in each of the countries. Within the Middle East, former European colonies Syria, Egypt, Iraq, Yemen, and the Sudan all embraced the cause of communism, and would receive technical assistance, weapons as well as financial assistance by the Soviet Union. Some of these countries maintained their friendly relationships to their counterparts in the Soviet Union and communism didn't perform well for all of them. However, they did use Soviet aid to break the dominance of Western imperial powerhouses. This way they posed a threat to capitalism's global war against communism.

Cold War as Economic War

Every war when they last enough, will eventually turn into battles between opposing economic systems. Which side is able to take on more troops and replace them? Which side is able to support them with better and more powerful weapons and equipment? Which one can provide support to its civilians while fighting in a continuous manner? What side is better equipped to equip and empower allies to fight place? In the same way that the Cold War was one of ideas, weapons strategies, concepts, and ideas the Cold War was a direct battle between two completely different economic system.

The system that was communist in the Soviet Union relied on central government planning to make economic decisions and incentives that were given to groups. The capitalist system of United States used diffuse, market-based decision-making processes and personal self-interest to motivate employees. This was the primary ideological conflict that characterized that Cold War. In the end, the U.S. system won hands down.

U.S. leaders believed from the beginning that capitalism was superior to the communist system. They devised policies and institutions that were a reflection of this belief, and took the War into economic battlegrounds across the globe. In the Marshall Plan, Marshall Plan poured $13 billion into Europe to aid in the rebuilding of Europe from the devastation of World War II. It was the International Monetary Fund and the World Bank provided Western-leaning countries with currency reserves, loans and technical assistance for the development of resources, industrial agriculture, and other systems. The "economic marvels" that occurred in Japan, Germany, Korea as well as Taiwan have been as political triumphs during the Cold War as they were success in the economy of their respective populations. They demonstrated that capitalism "delivered its goods" but no comparable examples could achieve the same level of success as communism.

The Western economy proved to be superior over that of the Soviet system that by the year 1960, West Germany had not just recovered from the destruction from World War II, it produced more than all Europe's economies Eastern Europe combined! In the final year in the Cold War, thirty years after the war it was believed that we in the U.S. would be outspending the Soviets three-to-one on military terms while outperforming them five-to-1 in economic terms. More than megatons and missiles the vast increase in economic production that ultimately took the victory in victory in the Cold War for the West.

Arms Races

The race to determine which side could construct the most sophisticated weapon systems was an integral part during the Cold War. The "arms race" as it was referred to was actually started with the U.S. Manhattan Project to build the nuclear bomb. The arms race came in various different forms. The initial focus was on the destructive potential from the guns themselves.

Atom (A) bombs changed for hydrogen (H) bombs. Small H-bombs then were transformed into huge H-bombs. The 15 kiloton "Fat Man" A-bomb that hit Hiroshima was soon dwarfed by the 20-30and 40-megaton H-bombs in the 1950s' final years bombs that proved thousands of years stronger. More destructive power was employed to counteract the inaccuracy that delivery trucks had.

Delivery systems themselves were an important aspect in the race for arms. In the beginning, bombs were meant to be delivered via airplanes--bombers. Later, propeller-driven aircrafts were jet-powered. Then nuclear warheads were put on top of missiles. Then, the missiles were positioned on railroad cars in order to make them unaffected. They were later equipped with multiple warheads, which could be targeted at various places.

In addition to ballistic missiles (those that flew throughout space) were further added short-range missiles that soared hundreds of feet higher than the ground and could hit their targets in a matter of minutes. This resulted in a frightening "launch after warning" obligation wherein the situation of a warning both sides were required to "use the missiles or risk losing the ability to use them." The accuracy of missiles was increased to the point where they could travel across the globe and even land within a few 100 yards of their targets. In the seemingly endless search for an advantage.

In addition, to destructive technology and delivery systems, the war on arms was centered around the sheer number. In the final days of Cold War, the U.S. was home to more than thirty thousand nuclear warheads using a mix of land, air or sea-based weapons. In contrast, the Soviet Union possessed some 40,000 weapons, based on the same range in delivery methods. As even a few hundred weapons, if destroyed could have killed everyone on earth in a matter of seconds, the logic behind the arms race was nearly clinically insane. This insanity and the horror it caused on generations of Earth's people that are among the most enduring legacy from the Cold War.

Brutal Communist Repression

The Soviet Union was a brutal police state. Many of the countries that became part of the orbit of its "satellites," were police states too, particularly those that were part of Eastern Europe. The majority of communist leaders were able to stay in power by brutally suppressing their own citizens, employing their armies to keep law and order and massive police forces within the country to monitor their citizens. The dissidents of the Soviet Union were sent to prison camps in Siberia which were referred to as "Gulags."

The Soviet Union encouraged its puppet states to employ similar tactics to their own citizens. In 1956, as the citizens of Hungary began to revolt against oppressive Soviet-backed government in Hungary, they were repelled by the Soviet Union sent tanks to Budapest which was the capital of Hungary to crush the uprising. The situation in East Germany, so many people were fleeing towards in the West that in 1961 , the communist government was forced to construct a wall, the Berlin Wall, to confine them within their country. In 1968, when citizens of Czechoslovakia protested against communist rule they were punished with exactly the same Soviet tanks and state-controlled violence that had stopped the revolt in Hungary 12 years earlier.

This and similar actions in other countries of communism exposed what was true about Soviet and in the following years, Chinese regimes: they were simply dictatorships disguised as "peoples republics." Mao Zedong, the chief of the communist China exposed this truth by introducing a slogan for the revolution: "Power comes from the barrel of gun."

Chapter 13: The Collapse Of The Soviet Bloc

One of the faults that afflicted one of the biggest flaws in Soviet system was its acceptance of communism. In communism property was owned as a common property, not owned through private people. This was a deprivation of personal motivations that guide the behavior of the capitalist system. Additionally, its central planning system obfuscated the demand and supply signals that are the basis markets. This caused massive distortions in distribution and production as well as massive economic waste. Communism was also not able to innovate in the field of new technology, specifically electronic devices, a new technological paradigm that is being developed within the West.

Due to these flaws that led to the collapse of the communist regime, it became increasingly less productive, and therefore, less competitive. Essential consumer goods such as cars and appliances for the home were always being sold out. The range of goods available was limited, and the quality of goods was not high. The economy failed to generate enough revenue to support the investment levels which boost productivity. The vast sums of money were allocated to the military in order to keep pace with the defense spending in the U.S. The result of all these factors was economic stagnation even a regress.

In the meantime, Soviet governments maintained power through coercion, force and intimidation. This wasn't just a matter of those in the Soviet Union proper, but to the regimes that were in the power of its satellite and clients states. The governments of these states were able to spy on their citizens and censored media in all forms, and brutally suppressed any protest or criticism and incarcerated or executed dissidents. Communist administrations also had a reputation for corruption and many of their decisions were not taken out of consideration for the interests of the state or market requirements however, due to the bribe system, which was prevalent at all levels of the government. These factors led to a huge resentment of the people of their society and government.

In the 1980s, the U.S. undertook a massive military expansion under the presidency that of Ronald Reagan. U.S. military spending had declined in the wake of the U.S. defeat in Vietnam. Reagan's intention was to re-invigorate military expenditures in order to devastate the Soviets by requiring them shift increasing amounts of their national production towards the army. One particular program was not only an economic threat, but also a major military risk to Soviet Union. Ronald Reagan's Strategic Defense Initiative (SDI) would have nuclear warheads launch offensively at the Soviets from space. The Soviets could not respond to this formidable combination of military and economic threats.

In 1981, workers at the shipyard at Gdansk, Poland staged a labor strike in protest of pay as well as working conditions. With help from the Soviet Union, the government was unable to stop the uprising and the protests spread rapidly across the country. It was forced to recognize the worker the union, Solidarity, and to provide it with a place in the formulation of national policy. The Solidarity's achievements were praised all over Eastern Europe as the proper example of how workers should be treated as well as how governments should be engaging their citizens. It could be the beginning of the end of this Soviet system.

In 1985 the newly elected Soviet president, Mikhail Gorbachev, came to power in 1985. He was called an exemplary "Superman" because he had risen within the Communist Party more quickly than any other person in the time of the nation. He was well-educated and charismatic, vivacious and focused. Gorbachev acknowledged his country's Soviet Union was backwards and losing influence in comparison with the U.S. He immediately began an effort to improve the society, including its economy and the government. He implemented two programs that could become signature, but accidentally fatally innovative ideas.

"Perestroika" is Gorbachev's attempt to reform the economy to improve its productivity and make it in line in comparison to the West. One of the main features in Perestroika was the transfer of economic decision-making out the control of Moscow and into regionally-managed, dispersed companies. The government also stopped providing subsidies for unprofitable businesses, such as large factories and cooperatives for agriculture. In addition, it opened a number of market to the competition of businesses from the West. The totality of these moves resulted in a massive upset to the Soviet economy. They were resisted with a ferocious stance by the conservative forces of the society.

The second reform plan was dubbed "Glasnost," or "Openness." Glasnost encouraged "more light" and increased participation in civic activities by the population. Gorbachev eliminated many of the older corrupt government officials out of the most senior levels of the government. The voices of the dissidents in the populace were tolerated , and a lively underground of artists, intellectuals and activists emerged nearly in a matter of hours, voicing harsh criticism about and criticism of the Soviet system. Gorbachev himself had criticized Stalin for the excesses he committed in the 1930s, such as purges that killed millions. Like Perestroika, Glasnost was deeply rejected and disapproved of by old-fashioned conservatives who believed it was a threat to their position of privilege.

Conclusion

The Cuban Missile Crisis showed the massive change the world experienced after the end in World War Two. It was the Crisis came the nearest the world ever came towards nuclear conflict. It is impossible that US would have let the Crisis to last much more time, and if they had struck Cuba and not require nuclear missiles located within the USSR to begin the nuclear war. Although it was not known in people in the US during the period the existence of nukes in Cuba and they were readily available to be used if the US were to attack Cuba.

The world was not in a position to get to a point that the superpowers were so near to nuclear conflict. It was the events in the period following World War Two ended in Europe that created an uneasy world by two countries: the USA as well as the USSR. The superpowers were unable reach a post-war agreement for Europe which was in their mutual favor and began to look at one another through a different lens. This distrust increased and by 1949 both had influence in Europe that they wanted to protect. It was the

USSR developed economies operate on the same lines as their communist system, whereas the USA employed its Marshall Plan to support capitalist democracies which would later be part of the international trading system. Events in 1949 and through the 1950s pushed the two sides further separated. The expansion to China to the side of communism caused the US to be more concerned that communism could take over East Asia, further encouraging the US to join the Korean War. In the end, Korean War itself contributed to the militarization of the West while since the super-powers were investing massively on nuclear arsenals. The superpowers both wanted remain one step ahead of the competition and had more advanced technology in nuclear that could threaten the territory of the other. This culminated in the most powerful nuclear test that the globe has ever witnessed in 1961.

It was this path of remilitarization, animosity along with nuclear developments that brought about an eventual Cuban Missile Crisis.

The next phase of Cold War would see more drastic modifications. The relationship between the superpowers was tense through in the 1970s as well as 1960s with times improving, and at other times getting worse. The advancement of nuclear technology was not stopped however, there were also attempts to control arms. It was a time when the Cold War also expanded into new territories, and trouble was raging in certain territories which were already part of during the Cold War. Vietnam, Angola, Czechoslovakia, Egypt, and Afghanistan are only a few regions that were to become Cold War battle-zones in this time.

The threat of nuclear war was prevented in 1962, however the world was in the midst of a new type of conflict. The superpowers were still learning to manage in a volatile world close to nuclear catastrophe.

www.ingramcontent.com/pod-product-compliance
Lightning Source LLC
Chambersburg PA
CBHW050401120526
44590CB00015B/1785